D3181
320

D1192179

Historic Architecture of the Royal Navy

An Introduction

Historic Architecture of the Royal Navy

An Introduction

J. G. COAD

London
Victor Gollancz Ltd
1983

For Jennifer

© J. G. Coad 1983

British Library Cataloguing in Publication Data
Coad, Jonathan
    Historic architecture of the Royal Navy.
    1.Navy-yards and naval stations—Great Britain—
    History
    I. Title
    623′.64′0941   VA460.A1

    ISBN 0-575-03277-4

Designed by Harold Bartram

Filmset and printed in Great Britain by
BAS Printers Limited, Over Wallop, Hampshire

Contents

List of Illustrations   6

List of Maps and Plans   10

Foreword   11

Preface and Acknowledgements   13

Introduction   15

1   Naval Bases   17

2   Building and Maintaining the Fleet   41

3   Manufacturing within the Dockyards   60

4   Naval Warehouses   83

5   Boundaries, Houses, Churches and Schools   93

6   Provisioning the Fleet   114

7   Arming the Warships   129

8   Naval Hospitals   142

Sources   154

Sources of Illustrations   156

Index   157

List of Illustrations

Chapter 1

1   Chatham Dockyard in the 1690s.
2   Chatham Dockyard c 1710.
3   Plymouth Dockyard in 1698.
4   Plymouth Dockyard c 1800.
5   Devonport Dockyard. The Officers' Terrace today.
6   Portsmouth Dockyard in the early eighteenth century.
7   Plymouth Dockyard 1698. The Tarring and Yarn Houses.
8   Sheerness in 1774.
9   Part of Portsmouth Dockyard in 1774.
10 The southern end of Chatham in 1774.
11 Portsmouth Dockyard firemen, c 1900, in front of the water tower.
12 Portsmouth Dockyard. The first steam engine to be used by the navy in 1797.
13 Chatham Dockyard c 1804.
14 Minorca, Port Mahon naval base in the early eighteenth century.
15 Gibraltar Dockyard in the late 1880s.
16 Malta. The former dockyard in 1972.
17 Malta Dockyard in 1804.
18 Antigua Dockyard.
19 Port Royal, Jamaica, in 1897.
20 HMS *Achilles* nearing completion at Chatham in 1863.
21 Malta. The new factory nearing completion in 1887.
22 Expansion of Portsmouth Dockyard c 1910.
23 The north end of Portsmouth Dockyard about 75 years ago.
24 Portsmouth. An early twentieth-century view of the Steam Basin, now No 2 Basin.
25 Portsmouth Dockyard coaling point in 1908.
26 Bermuda victualling yard.

Chapter 2

27 Devonport. The only eighteenth-century slip remaining in a royal dockyard.
28 A ship on the stocks at Deptford by John Cleveley, painted in the 1770s.
29 Chatham Dockyard. The mast houses and mould loft begun in 1753.
30 Chatham Dockyard. Axonometric view of the mast house and mould loft.

31 Chatham Dockyard. The 1723 storehouse.

32 Antigua Dockyard sawpits.

33 Sheerness Dockyard. Joiners' shop, mould loft and sawpits.

34 Chatham Dockyard. Timber seasoning sheds on the 1774 model.

35 Chatham Dockyard: eighteenth-century seasoning sheds.

36 Devonport Dockyard. The 1770s' slip with its later timber roof.

37 Portsmouth Dockyard. A drawing of 1838 showing sections of a proposed timber roof.

38 Chatham Dockyard's unique range of covered slips.

39 Portsmouth Dockyard. The interior of the pioneer metal slip roofs before demolition in 1979.

40 Portsmouth Dockyard. Dummer's pioneer scheme of 1690 for a stone stepped dry-dock and two wet-docks.

41 Portsmouth Dockyard. No 1 Basin and dry-docks.

42 Plymouth Dockyard. Part of the 1774 model showing a double dock.

43 Chatham Dockyard. An aerial view of the basins taken in May 1982.

44 Portsmouth Dockyard. No 1 dock.

45 Portsmouth Dockyard. Part of Dummer's elaborate design for dock pumping in the 1690s.

46 The last naval treadwheel crane, formerly in use in Harwich dockyard.

47 Portsmouth Dockyard. The first dock pump to be powered by a steam engine.

48 Decoration on the stern of HMS *Victory*.

Chapter 3

49 Portsmouth Dockyard. The boat pond and 5, 6 and 7 boathouses.

50 Portsmouth Dockyard. Inside 7 boathouse in 1981.

51 Portsmouth Dockyard. Inside 6 boathouse.

52 Chatham Dockyard. The end of the Lower Boat Store.

53 Portsmouth Dockyard. One of a set of workshops and stores built 1786–1790.

54 Portsmouth Dockyard. The original 1780's design for a storehouse and workshops.

55 A scene inside the Devonport masthouse at the end of the nineteenth century.

56 Iron knees in the frigate *Unicorn*.

57 The construction of huge iron anchors.

58 Chatham Smithery. Edward Holl's 1806 design.

59 Smiths' shop at Antigua.

60 Chatham Dockyard. A plan of the proposed brick sail loft built in the 1720s.

61 At work in Chatham sail loft in 1981.

62 Bales of sisal inside the 1728 hemp house at Chatham in December 1981.

63 At work in the Chatham spinning room c 1900.

64 Portsmouth Dockyard. The late-eighteenth-century covered way connecting the hemp house and hatchelling house on the right with the 1770 double ropehouse.

65 Portsmouth double ropehouse photographed in 1942 before modernisation.

66 Devonport Dockyard. A cross-section of the spinning house in 1815.

67 Devonport Dockyard. The ropeyard as rebuilt between 1763 and 1771.

68 An aerial view of the southern end of Chatham Dockyard in 1982.

69 The laying floor at Chatham ropery, shortly before the end of Ministry of Defence production in 1983.

70 The Chatham yarn houses in 1799.

71 Devonport Dockyard. Capstans in the roof space of one of the black yarn houses.

72 One end of the Chatham ropehouse in the early nineteenth century.

73 A forming machine delivered to Chatham ropery in 1811.

74 Portsmouth Dockyard. The Block Mills built between 1802 and 1806.

75 Brunel's cornering saws for ships' blocks at Portsmouth.

76 Brunel's saw for *lignum vitae* sheeves for blocks.

77 Brunel's sawmill at Chatham.

78 The Chatham lead and paint mill.

79 Portsmouth 2 Ship Shop, completed in 1848.

Chapter 4

80 Plymouth Dockyard. The Great Storehouse of 1692.

81 The cordage house and tar cellars built at Chatham in 1718.

82 The Chatham clocktower building on the 1774 dockyard model at the National Maritime Museum.

83 Portsmouth Dockyard. 9, 10 and 11 Stores.

84 Portsmouth Dockyard. 10 Store, the 1776 drawing.

85 Portsmouth Dockyard: inside 10 Store.

86 A detail of the staircases inside 19 Store at Portsmouth.

87 Storehouses at Plymouth, roughly contemporary with 9, 10 and 11 Stores at Portsmouth.

88 Naval storehouses: part of the 1774 Plymouth model.

89 One of the earliest fireproof buildings: the former pay office at Portsmouth.

90 A 1793 design for the nothernmost of the Anchor Wharf storehouses at Chatham.

91 Sheerness. The great Quadrangle Storehouse.

92 Sheerness Boatstore.

Chapter 5

93 Portsmouth Dockyard. The Main Gate and dockyard wall completed in 1712.

94 Chatham Dockyard. The dockyard entrance built in 1719.

95 Chatham Dockyard. One of the wall towers contemporary with the Main Gate.

96 Chatham Dockyard. Wall towers contemporary with the Main Gate.

97 Antigua Dockyard. The eighteenth-century gateway and part of the boundary wall.

98 Plymouth Dockyard. The terrace designed in 1692 for the commissioner and twelve senior dockyard officers.

99 Plymouth Dockyard. The Commissioner's house in 1831.

100 Portsmouth Dockyard terrace. Design for the 1719 terrace.

101 Portsmouth Dockyard terrace today.

102 Chatham: early design for the existing terrace of twelve houses.

103 The centre of the Georgian dockyard at Chatham in May 1982.

104 Chatham Dockyard. The Commissioner's House.

105 Chatham Dockyard. The painted ceiling at the head of the main staircase in the Commissioner's House.

106 The former Commissioner's House at Portsmouth, now Admiralty House.

107 Gibraltar. The former Commissioner's House.

108 Antigua Dockyard. The early nineteenth-century quarters built to accomodate naval officers.

109 Antigua. Clarence House.

110 Antigua Dockyard. The Naval Officer's and Storekeeper's House.

111 Malta. The officers' terrace overlooking Dockyard Creek.

112 Bermuda. The main elevation of the Commissioner's House.

113 Portsmouth. St Ann's Church.

114 Chatham. Holl's 1805 design for the dockyard chapel.

115 Chatham: the interior of the chapel.

116 Portsmouth. The Naval Academy of 1729, now the Staff Officers' Mess.

117 Portsmouth. The former School for Naval Architecture.

118 Unicorn Gate, Portsmouth.

Chapter 6

119 Cooperage buildings of 1766 in the former Weevil Victualling Yard, Gosport.

120 The grand entrance to the Royal William Victualling Yard, Stonehouse.

121 The heart of the Royal William Yard.

122 Rennie's brewery at Royal William Yard.

123 Royal William Yard. Part of the interior of Melville Square.

124 Royal William Yard. One of the granite staircases to the main offices.

125 Royal William Yard. Houses for the senior victualling officers.

126 Royal Clarence Victualling Yard. The main entrance from the inside.

127 Royal Clarence Yard in 1898.

128 Royal Clarence Yard. The mill/bakery in 1969.

129 Gibraltar Victualling Yard.

130 Part of the interior of the Gibraltar storehouse.
131 The mill/bakery at Dockyard Creek, Malta.

Chapter 7
132 1777 design for a pair of gunpowder magazines at Priddy's Hard Alverstoke.
133 Priddy's Hard, Alverstoke, showing two proposed magazines.
134 Powder magazines at Purfleet on the Essex bank of the Thames.
135 Inside one of the Purfleet powder magazines.
136 The 1770 powder magazine at Priddy's Hard.
137 The tiny basin at Priddy's Hard.
138 Chatham. Upnor Castle.
139 The main ordnance wharf at Chatham; early eighteenth-century warehouses demolished after the Second World War.
140 Polishing cannon balls at Morice Ordnance Yard in 1855.
141 Morice yard, the Officers' Terrace completed in 1723.
142 One of the original storehouses at Morice Yard.
143 Nineteenth-century magazine at Bull Point on the Tamar.

Chapter 8
144 An early eighteenth-century view of the naval hospital, Minorca.
145 A ground floor ward in Mahon Hospital, Minorca.
146 An aerial view of Mahon hospital, Minorca.
147 Gibraltar. The old naval hospital.
148 Haslar Hospital, Gosport.
149 Haslar Hospital. The great courtyard.
150 The main entrance to Haslar hospital in 1942.
151 Stonehouse Hospital, Plymouth.
152 Stonehouse Hospital early this century.
153 Stonehouse Hospital. The 1763 terrace for the senior medical staff.
154 The former naval hospital, Malta, about 1860.

References in the text to illustrations are indicated by the plate number in heavy type.

List of Maps and Plans

page 14 Bases of the Royal Navy mentioned in the text.
Fig. 1   Portsmouth. Location map of naval and ordnance facilities. *page 22*
Fig. 2   Portsmouth Dockyard c 1700. *page 24*
Fig. 3   Portsmouth Dockyard c 1850. *page 27*
Fig. 4   Chatham Dockyard c 1850. *page 28*
Fig. 5   Devonport Dockyard c 1850. *page 33*
Fig. 6   Antigua Dockyard c 1800. *page 47*
Fig. 7   Royal William Victualling Yard c 1830. *page 120*
Fig. 8   Morice Ordnance Yard, Devonport. *page 134*
Fig. 9   Haslar Royal Naval Hospital c 1800. *page 147*
Buildings which survive are shown in solid black on the maps. Those that have vanished are shown in outline.

Foreword

by Admiral of the Fleet, Lord Lewin, KG, GCB, MVO, DSC

The achievements of the ships and men of the Royal Navy and the part they have played over the centuries in the security of the Realm and the foundation of Empire are well recorded in history. Not so well known is the complementary contribution made by the supporting dockyards and bases without which the far-flung fleets could not have been despatched or sustained. In this meticulously researched book, Jonathan Coad provides both a fascinating account and a valuable record of the complex organisation that was needed to fit out, store and arm the ships, and to care for the health of the men who manned them.

'Being in all respects ready for sea . . .'. So still runs the traditional opening phrase of the sailing orders given to the captain of a ship by his superior commander. The Navy relied on the dockyards to make the ships 'ready for sea'.

In the last 40 years the Royal Navy has made a transition more fundamental than the change from sail to steam. Nuclear propulsion and gas turbines have replaced the oil-fired boiler, guns have given way to missiles; even the hammock that served the sailor for 400 years has been entirely replaced by the bunk. Operationally the fleet no longer has to rely on a chain of overseas bases but can patrol and fight thousands of miles from home for many months, as recent events have shown.

Here in the United Kingdom the historic dockyards have had to be adapted for the support of this new navy. Many of the fine old buildings that served the fleet so well in the past are unsuitable for modern purposes or, like Chatham Dockyard, are no longer required. This book, which describes so well the part they have played in our history, is a timely reminder that they are as much a part of our maritime heritage as HMS *Victory* herself.

Lewin of Greenwich

Admiral of the Fleet

Preface and Acknowledgements

This book is intended as an introduction to the architecture of the Royal Navy. Not the naval architecture of warships but the naval architecture of the royal dockyards and associated facilities that served and made possible the former and in so doing shaped much of Great Britain's modern history.

The book is not an exhaustive survey but it aims to draw attention to the more notable surviving architecture and engineering works in the home and overseas naval bases and to say something about the administrative organisations and social and military pressures which created and sustained them. It is the distillation of a much larger and as such more comprehensive manuscript and I am very grateful to Victoria Petrie-Hay and Victor Gollancz Ltd for commissioning this abbreviated version.

This is the result of some fifteen years of intermittent research, together with help from a great many people and organisations. Visits to the Mediterranean bases were made possible through the generosity of the Leverhulme Trust, those to Bermuda, Antigua and St Lucia with help from the British Academy. In Chatham, Portsmouth, Devonport, Malta, Gibraltar and Bermuda I have received a great deal of assistance and kindness from naval and civilian staff. My visits to Port Mahon were made through the courtesy of the Spanish Ministry of Marine, visits to the former Malta dockyard through the courtesy of the Malta Dry Docks Co., Sheerness by courtesy of the Medway Ports' Authority, and the old part of Bermuda base by courtesy of the Bermuda Maritime Trust. I am very grateful to all these organisations and people, as well as to the staff of the Public Record Office, British Library (Map Room and Department of Manuscripts) and especially to the staff of the National Maritime Museum.

It is perhaps invidious to name individuals when so many have been so generous with their time and knowledge, but Mr A. W. H. Pearsall and Dr R. J. B. Knight of the National Maritime Museum have been especially useful with their help and advice. I have also received much help from Mr J. Maps (Minorca), Mr D. Nicholson (Antigua) and Mr and Mrs R. Sturdy (Bermuda) whose kindness and hospitality were limitless. To everyone I am deeply grateful, but at the end of the day any mistakes remain my responsibility.

J. G. Coad

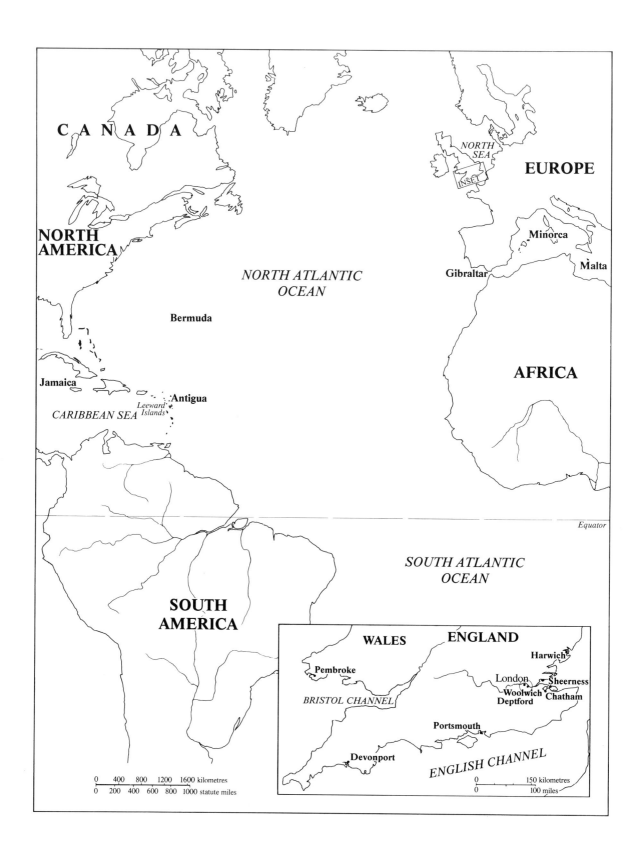

C A N A D A

NORTH
AMERICA

NORTH ATLANTIC
OCEAN

Bermuda

Jamaica

CARIBBEAN SEA

Leeward
Islands

Antigua

NORTH
SEA

INSET

EUROPE

Minorca

Malta

Gibraltar

AFRICA

Equator

SOUTH ATLANTIC
OCEAN

SOUTH
AMERICA

WALES

ENGLAND

Harwich

Pembroke

London

Sheerness

BRISTOL CHANNEL

Woolwich
Deptford

Chatham

Portsmouth

Devonport

ENGLISH CHANNEL

| 0 | 400 | 800 | 1200 | 1600 | kilometres |

| 0 | 200 | 400 | 600 | 800 | 1000 | statute miles |

| 0 | | 150 | kilometres |

| 0 | | 100 | miles |

14

Introduction

The Royal Navy is unique among armed services of the Crown in the length of time it has occupied its main bases. Such long continuity has led to a remarkable accumulation of naval buildings and engineering works of great historic, architectural and engineering interest. Before the Industrial Revolution of the mid-eighteenth century, the royal dockyards could lay claim to being the industrial centres of England, if not perhaps in terms of absolute numbers, certainly in the variety of crafts and trades to be found in them or closely associated with them. Even now, they remain major industrial enterprises.

If naval exploits have tended to capture the attention of historians and journalists, these exploits depended absolutely upon the ability of the royal dockyards and the ordnance and victualling yards to build, equip and sustain the fleet. Lacking the glamour of the fleet itself, the image of shore establishments for long tended to be one of inefficiency and corruption—yet this is far from a balanced picture for they were often in the van of technical progress. At the end of the seventeenth century Edward Dummer pioneered stepped stone dry-docks at Portsmouth and Plymouth. Half a century later, modernisation of these two yards, in the words of the Earl of Sandwich, First Lord of the Admiralty, made them superior to anything in Europe. At the end of the eighteenth century Marc Isambard Brunel was employed to build a blockmills at Portsmouth—the first instance in the world of the use of machine tools for mass-production—and he later designed a remarkable sawmill at Chatham. The Rennies, father and son, played notable parts at Plymouth and Sheerness as well as advising on Bermuda, while in the mid-nineteenth century in collaboration with the Royal Engineers, the royal dockyards pioneered the use of large-span metal roofs. Victualling and ordnance yards and naval hospitals likewise have their own interests and histories, while from the early eighteenth century Admiralty and Navy Boards wrestled with problems of creating and maintaining bases in the Mediterranean, Caribbean and North America.

From the sixteenth century until challenged by the development of the aeroplane, the royal dockyards were the heart of the country's defence effort. Behind their high walls they represented the government's greatest continuing capital investment in protection of the realm. Security has meant that few apart from those working for the navy have seen the dockyards, but they have rarely failed to impress the intelligent visitor, as the writings of Daniel Defoe in the 1720s and Charles Dickens nearly a century and a half later testify. Iron Age hill camps, Roman coastal forts, medieval castles and then artillery defences—the last usually to protect naval bases—provide abundant evidence for these islands' military history. In the same way the buildings and engineering works of the royal dockyards are tangible witness to Great Britain's once formidable maritime supremacy.

The modern navy effectively begins with Henry VII and his son, but the earliest surviving dockyard building dates from the 1690s. For this reason this book concentrates on the period 1700 to 1850, a time covering the classic age of the sailing navy, the time of its global expansion and many of its greatest victories. By the 1850s steam-powered warships were already part of the navy, but even so the fleet which sailed to the Crimea in 1854 superficially differed little from that which had fought at Trafalgar in 1805. Within a very few years, development of rifled ordnance and the all-metal armoured warship had totally transformed the Royal Navy and with it the major dockyards which had vast extensions to accommodate the boiler shops, foundries and machine shops needed to cope with the new technology. This book touches briefly on these later developments, all of which are notable for their civil engineering but possibly less so for their contribution to dockyard architecture.

This century a combination of dockyard closures, war damage and modernisation has effected great changes. The old heart of Devonport was virtually destroyed in 1941 and 1942, while Portsmouth was badly damaged. Yet much survives in the home bases: Devonport still has its former ordnance yard and Royal William Victualling Yard; Portsmouth has Haslar Royal Naval Hospital and Priddy's Hard. Pride of place among dockyards must go to Chatham, its old end still a virtually intact Georgian dockyard, its numerous buildings—architecturally, good bad and indifferent—a memorial to and part of the explanation for the navy of Vernon, Howe and Nelson. Chatham dockyard closes in 1984. If this book serves to introduce naval shore architecture to a wider audience, it will have served its purpose.

The book's format has not allowed for references. Most of the information comes from primary source material held in the Public Record Office and the National Maritime Museum. A list of the principal classes of documents consulted, together with relevant published works will be found at the end of the book.

Chapter 1
Naval Bases

The royal dockyards were created to build and maintain the ships of the Royal Navy. Associated with them were victualling yards, ordnance yards and, later, naval hospitals. Frequently the butt of criticism, not all of it merited, the naval shore establishments underpinned Great Britain's maritime power and were barometers of empire. Without them there could have been no Royal Navy. Permanent royal dockyards were a creation of the Tudor monarchs. Portsmouth was developing at the end of the fifteenth century, Woolwich and Deptford soon after; Chatham was founded in 1547. Later, Sheerness was built at the mouth of the Medway and at the end of the seventeenth century Plymouth Dock, renamed Devonport in 1823, was laid out in response to Britain's growing commercial and strategic interests in the Mediterranean and across the Atlantic. After Plymouth Dock only two more home dockyards were established: in the early nineteenth century Pembroke was founded as a shipbuilding yard and a hundred years later Rosyth was rapidly built in response to the growing naval power of Imperial Germany.

Until the end of the seventeenth century warships were rarely at sea during winter. As autumn days shortened and weather deteriorated, they returned to the dockyards for overhaul and for crews to be paid off. Indeed, Tudor and Stuart royal finances were such that frequently the fleet could swing idly on its mooring for years, rot eating out the hearts of ships, crews unpaid and dockyards empty of stores. But well before the end of the seventeenth century, England's commitments overseas were growing. Settlers in New England, plantation owners in the Caribbean, merchants in the Mediterranean all demanded naval protection. While this could be provided in the summer, it was an increasingly unsatisfactory arrangement. As early as the winter of 1656–7 Blake had kept his fleet abroad and overhauled it at Lisbon. In the 1690s Russell repeated this considerable feat at Cadiz, but logistics were formidable and depended on friendly European neighbours.

1. Chatham Dockyard. Part of the Stuart residences and storehouses in the centre of the yard. At the time of this survey in the 1690s Chatham was still the premier naval base, something not apparent from the domestic scale of these buildings.

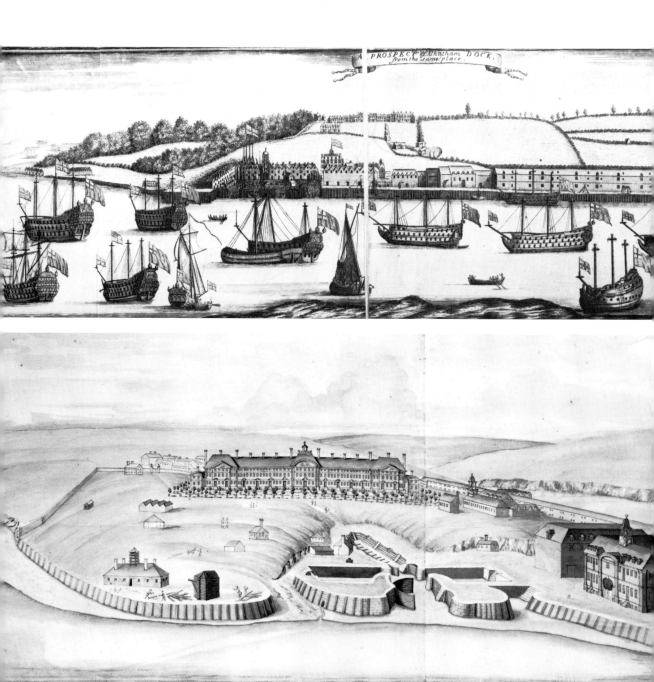

2. *Top* Chatham Dockyard c. 1710. The heart of the Stuart yard is the all-important complex of docks and building slips. The commissioner's new house (plate 104) lies to the right of these and is flying the Union flag. On the extreme right is the pedimented range of storehouses on Ordnance Wharf. The background is still rural, although some 49 years later the hill was to be crowned with a powerful defensive work—the Chatham Lines—designed to protect the dockyard.

3. *Above* Plymouth Dockyard in 1698. Dummer's view shows England's newest dockyard nearing completion, its short-lived spaciousness contrasting with Chatham. To the right is the great storehouse in

18

front of the long buildings of the ropery. Overlooking the dry and wet docks is the imposing officers' terrace, one of the earliest terraces to be designed to have an architectural unity.

The solution adopted by the Royal Navy from the early eighteenth century was to create its own overseas bases. Here stores and workshop facilities could be to hand, ships could be careened, victuals stockpiled and crews allowed ashore. In the creation of these Great Britain was far in advance of her European rivals. As the British Empire grew, naval bases studded the globe like well-placed sentry-boxes. In 1704 Gibraltar was captured, but a far more important acquisition came four years later with the surrender of Minorca with its superb natural harbour at Mahon. Across the Atlantic, Port Royal and Port Antonio in Jamaica, English Harbour in Antigua and Halifax in Nova Scotia were developed with the assistance of colonists eager to have the comforting sight of British warships. Malta followed in 1800 and Bermuda at roughly the same time, the latter establishment one result of the American War of Independence. As the empire expanded, bases followed the fleet: Esquimault, Simonstown, St Lucia, Aden, Madras, Bombay, Trincomalee. As Lutyens and Baker laboured on the creation of New Delhi, that final and short-lived flowering of the capital of British India, Admiralty architects and engineers were busy on the expansion of the great naval base at Singapore, destined to have almost as short a life under the British flag. Half a century on from expansion of Singapore dockyard, shrinking of responsibilities and determination leaves only Devonport and Rosyth, with Portsmouth and Gibraltar set to become shadows of their former selves.

Historically, not all dockyards had the same functions. The name is a pointer to their original purpose and, in England, a prime reason for their longevity in the same locations. The first dry-dock was built at Henry VII's behest at Portsmouth in 1495. Not only was it very expensive, but it was also the first major piece of shore equipment owned by the navy. Dry-docks had to be carefully sited, sheltered from the surge and battering of storms yet close to deep water where there was a good rise and fall of tide to allow for gravity drainage. Such was the expense that not all home dockyards had them before the seventeenth century, but upon their location depended all else; they formed the very heart of the naval establishments. In the yard around the dock clustered all the other buildings and facilities.

Although dockyards were originally established to build and maintain the fleet, reasons of location led some to eclipse others in importance. What set these few apart was their use as bases by the fleet. To build and refit warships required just a dockyard; to be home to the fleet required other facilities: safe and sheltered moorings, ordnance yards, gunpowder stores, victualling yards and—eventually and long-overdue—naval hospitals. In the seventeenth century, the sheltered waters of the Medway and rivalry with the Dutch caused Chatham to become the first naval base with facilities more than for just a dockyard. In the eighteenth century changing strategic considerations led to the rise and predominance of Portsmouth and Plymouth; two centuries later Rosyth was to join this elite group. The smaller dockyards built and repaired ships, maintained reserves of stores

4. Plymouth Dockyard c. 1800. This painting by Pocock well illustrates the eighteenth-century growth of this western base. Dummer's terrace can be seen left of centre. Additional land acquired in the 1760s had been used for new storehouses, building slips, a smithery and ropery. This neat and orderly layout survived largely intact until 1941. In its Georgian heyday this was one of the best-equipped naval bases in Europe.

adequate to their tasks and played host to individual ships or small squadrons who might be based at them. Not having to lay up large numbers of ships into reserve—put them 'in ordinary'—they had no need for the great ranges of storehouses for equipment removed ashore for safekeeping.

The overseas bases were smaller versions of the home bases, but with the exception of Malta and the Indian yards in the nineteenth century, none of them ever built warships. More important, until Malta completed one in 1847, none had a dry-dock, although plans for a double one at Antigua were drawn up in 1795. In consequence, major refits remained the prerogative of home yards until late in the nineteenth century. External hull repairs at overseas yards were limited to what could be tackled on careen—the hauling down of a ship adjacent to the shore to expose one side of her hull, an operation always attended with some risk to the ship's safety. Simple repairs, sheltered anchorage, stores and provisions were the intended roles for overseas yards. But imperfect understanding of balanced diets, limited methods of food preservation, rudimentary hygiene and lengthening voyages combined to ensure that no overseas base lacked a hospital and well-filled naval cemetery. Indeed, naval hospitals appeared at overseas bases, most notably at Minorca, 40 years before a reluctant Admiralty agreed to shoulder the expense of navy-built and navy-run hospitals in England. By the early seventeenth century, the royal dockyards probably contained the largest concentration of industrial skills to be found in what was still a predominantly agricultural England. Shipwrights, joiners, house carpenters, painters, blacksmiths, anchor-smiths, sailmakers, ropemakers,

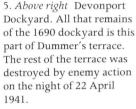

5. *Above right* Devonport Dockyard. All that remains of the 1690 dockyard is this part of Dummer's terrace. The rest of the terrace was destroyed by enemy action on the night of 22 April 1941.

riggers and numerous other smaller trades were to be found within their boundary walls, representing a great and continuing government investment.

While the Admiralty controlled the fleet and was responsible for its deployment, from 1660 to its abolition in 1832 the royal dockyards were under the control of the Navy Board. Similar boards ran the victualling yards, hospitals and ordnance yards, although the Board of Ordnance had wider responsibilities for both army and navy and was not abolished until May 1855.

Both Admiralty and Navy Board were based in London, but from the mid-seventeenth century the latter board began the practice of outstationing commissioners to take charge of the more important dockyards too far from London for direct supervision. Portsmouth, Chatham, Plymouth and Pembroke all had such outstationed board members, while overseas Halifax, Gibraltar and Malta were deemed of sufficient importance to warrant similar arrangements. At the other end of the scale, the smallest overseas yards were often in charge of a master shipwright or storekeeper who answered to the senior naval officer on station, an unsatisfactory administrative arrangement all too open to abuse.

Before 1795, very few naval buildings and installations were designed by professional architects. Within the dockyards the master shipwright was expected to draw up designs for new buildings, consulting with other senior yard officers and then submitting drawings to the Navy Board's surveyor in London. If these were approved (which they usually were)

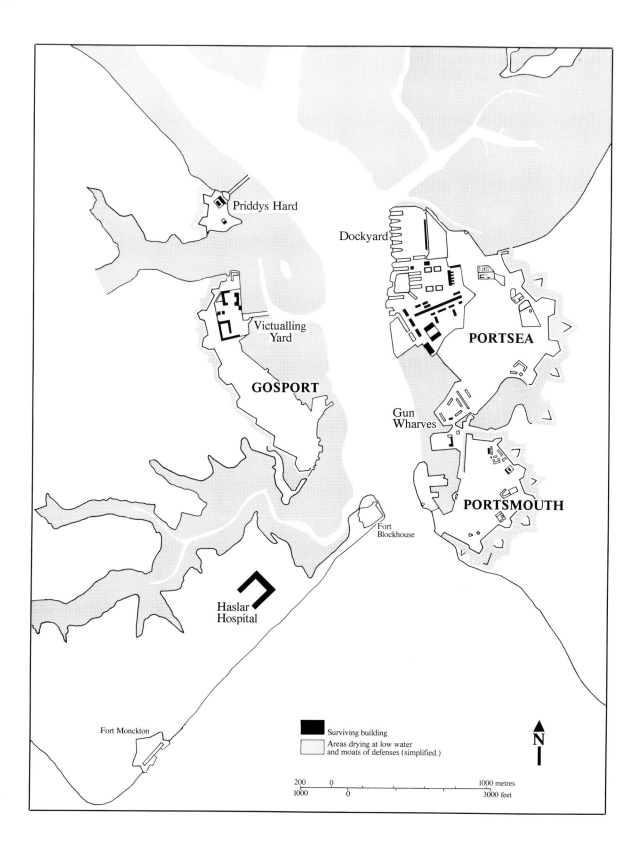

Priddys Hard

Dockyard

Victualling
Yard

PORTSEA

GOSPORT

Gun
Wharves

Fort
Blockhouse

PORTSMOUTH

Haslar
Hospital

Fort Monckton

■ Surviving building

☐ Areas drying at low water
and moats of defenses (simplified.)

200   0   1000 metres
1000   0   3000 feet

N

funds were allocated in the following year's estimates and the building was constructed. Only in very rare circumstances did any board employ an outside architect: Haslar and Stonehouse hospitals (149, 151) in the mid-eighteenth century and the commissioner's house at Portsmouth in 1785 were exceptions, the former probably on account of their size and specialised nature, the last because George III was a frequent visitor to Portsmouth and almost invariably stayed with the commissioner (106).

In 1795 the first and only Inspector General of Naval Works was appointed, charged with modernising and mechanising the dockyards. The holder, Brigadier-General Sir Samuel Bentham, brother of the better known Jeremy Bentham, had had a remarkable career in Russia and England and was to achieve some success in his new post. But his abrasive character and unfortunate method of appointment—his post was an Admiralty Board creation trespassing on the Navy Board's preserve—inevitably led to friction and he was not replaced after dismissal in 1812. But his small department lived on, although absorbed by the Navy Board, and amongst its members were the first professional architects to be permanently employed by the navy. The first architect was a shadowy figure called Samuel Bunce, but on his death in 1804 he was succeeded by Edward Holl who held the post for twenty years.

Initially, pressure of work was probably such that the architect could do little but endorse designs submitted to him. However, Holl speedily made his mark and was responsible for numerous surviving buildings, most apparent at Chatham, Sheerness where he worked with Rennie, Portsmouth and Bermuda. It is doubtful if he physically supervised construction of all his buildings, indeed he complained bitterly that his designs for Bermuda had been extensively and expensively altered locally, but he certainly established a style of simple dignified buildings, worthy successors

Fig. 1. Portsmouth. Location map of naval and ordnance facilities.

6. Portsmouth Dockyard in the early eighteenth century, its slips and storehouses prominent. Until the construction of the Plymouth breakwater in the 1820s, the Hampshire yard offered unrivalled safe mooring facilities.

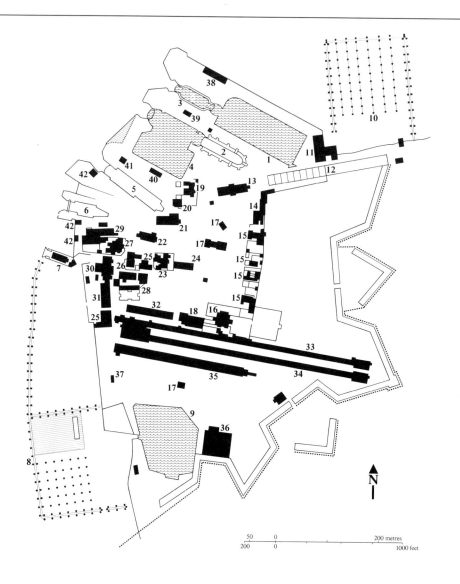

1. Upper Wet Dock
2. Great Stone Dock
3. Dry Dock
4. Great Basin
5. Double Dock
6. Building Slip
7. Hulk
8. New Mast Pond
9. Old Mast Pond
10. Boat Pond
11. Smithery
12. 22 Boathouses
13. New Storehouse
14. Stables
15. Officers' Houses (Store Keeper, Master Caulker, Builder's Assistant, Master Attendant)
16. Commissioner's House
17. Sawpits
18. Tarred Yarn House
19. Clerk of the Cheque's House
20. Office
21. Great Storehouse
22. Tap House
23. Clerk of the Survey's House
24. 5 Sawpits
25. Storehouse
26. Boatswain's House
27. Blockmaker's Shop
28. House Carpenters' Shop
29. Storehouses and Workshops
30. Blockstore
31. Pay Office
32. Hemp Store
33. Old Ropehouse
34. New Ropehouse
35. Long Storehouse
36. Mast House
37. Guardhouse
38. Broomhouse
39. Scavellmen's Cabin
40. Tar House
41. Old Dry Dock Pumphouse
42. Crane

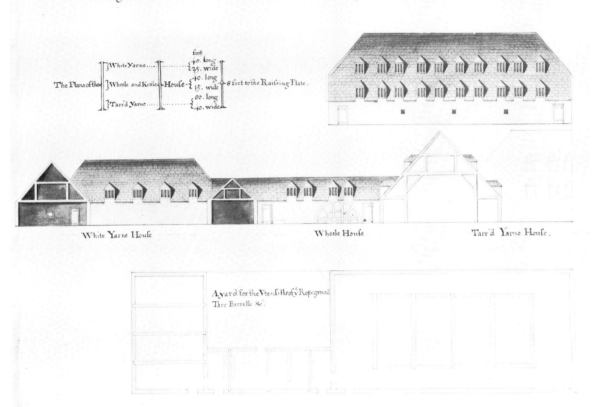

White Yarne House   Wheele House   Tarr'd Yarne House.

Fig. 2. Portsmouth Dockyard c. 1700.

7. Plymouth Dockyard 1698. This illustration of the ropery yarn houses shows the rare use of animal power in a dockyard, apart from hauling carts. The horse-driven wheel hauled white yarns through a tar kettle and into the black yarn house. Men were apparently often substituted for horses.

to those designed by the master shipwrights before him. From these early beginnings grew the enormous architects' departments of later years, but for much of the nineteenth century the Admiralty worked in close conjunction with the Royal Engineers whose skills were often peculiarly appropriate to the problems of construction in dockyards.

By the mid-eighteenth century it was established custom for the actual building work to be divided between the yard craftsmen and outside contractors. Then as now, dockyard bricklayers and house carpenters spent most of their time on maintenance and repairs, so in general they tended to construct only the smaller buildings which would not interrupt their normal routine too drastically. The largest projects were let to private contractors, sometimes London-based, who would establish offices at the main dockyard towns. In the second half of the eighteenth century the firm of Templar and Parlby, for example, seems to have monopolised the enormous works of expansion and reconstruction at Portsmouth and Plymouth, recruiting their labour from as far away as London. Sometimes, contractors and dockyard labour shared construction of buildings: 9, 10 and 11 Storehouses which flank the approach to HMS *Victory* and are home of the Portsmouth Royal Naval Museum had their vaulted basements built

Fig. 3. Portsmouth Dock-
yard c. 1850.

8. *Above right* Sheerness in
1774. When money and
land were in short supply
hulks were pressed into service. This illustration of
part of the contemporary
model at the National Maritime Museum shows the
extensive use of hulks as
stores and accommodation
for dockyard workmen.
Sheerness was never a
popular posting; this goes
far to explaining why.

9. *Right* Part of Portsmouth
Dockyard in 1774, showing
the spacious new buildings
then under construction.
The three handsome store-
houses in the centre still
survive (plate 83), as do
most of the buildings of the
ropery beyond. From the
contemporary model in the
National Maritime
Museum.

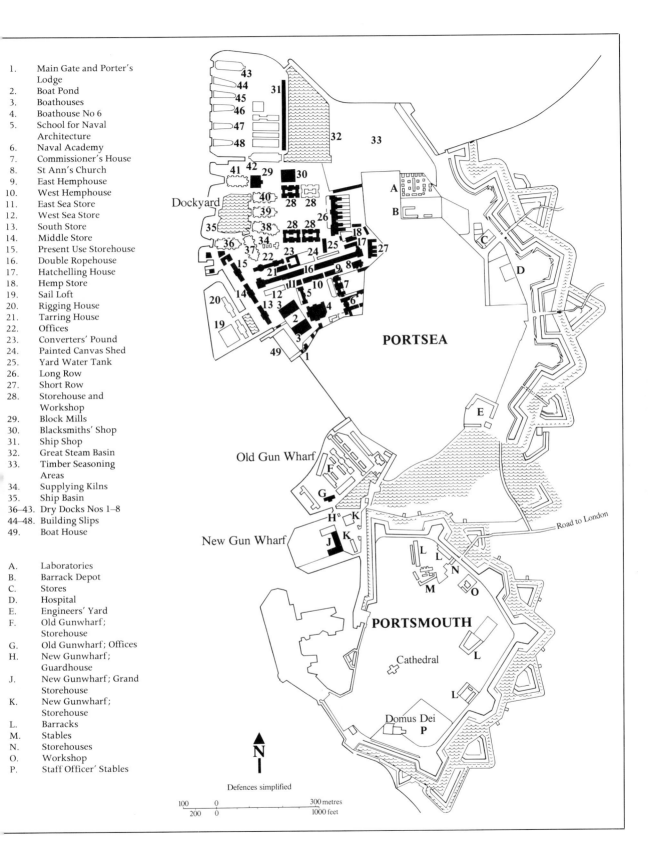

1. Main Gate and Porter's Lodge
2. Boat Pond
3. Boathouses
4. Boathouse No 6
5. School for Naval Architecture
6. Naval Academy
7. Commissioner's House
8. St Ann's Church
9. East Hemphouse
10. West Hemphouse
11. East Sea Store
12. West Sea Store
13. South Store
14. Middle Store
15. Present Use Storehouse
16. Double Ropehouse
17. Hatchelling House
18. Hemp Store
19. Sail Loft
20. Rigging House
21. Tarring House
22. Offices
23. Converters' Pound
24. Painted Canvas Shed
25. Yard Water Tank
26. Long Row
27. Short Row
28. Storehouse and Workshop
29. Block Mills
30. Blacksmiths' Shop
31. Ship Shop
32. Great Steam Basin
33. Timber Seasoning Areas
34. Supplying Kilns
35. Ship Basin
36–43. Dry Docks Nos 1–8
44–48. Building Slips
49. Boat House

A. Laboratories
B. Barrack Depot
C. Stores
D. Hospital
E. Engineers' Yard
F. Old Gunwharf; Storehouse
G. Old Gunwharf; Offices
H. New Gunwharf; Guardhouse
J. New Gunwharf; Grand Storehouse
K. New Gunwharf; Storehouse
L. Barracks
M. Stables
N. Storehouses
O. Workshop
P. Staff Officer' Stables

Dockyard

PORTSEA

Old Gun Wharf

New Gun Wharf

Road to London

PORTSMOUTH

Cathedral

Domus Dei

N

Defences simplified

100   0   300 metres
200   0   1000 feet

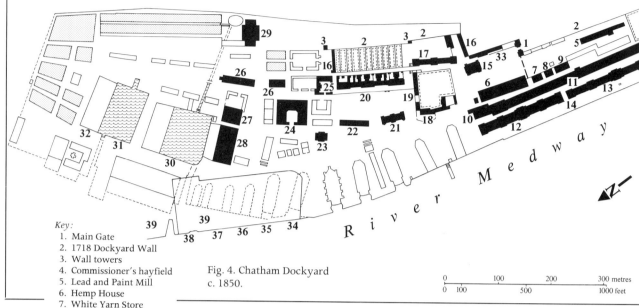

Key:
1. Main Gate
2. 1718 Dockyard Wall
3. Wall towers
4. Commissioner's hayfield
5. Lead and Paint Mill
6. Hemp House
7. White Yarn Store
8. Tarring House
9. Black Yarn Store
10. Hatchelling House
11. Ropery
12. Fitted Rigging House and
    Storehouse
13. No. 3 Storehouse
14. Anchor Wharf
15. Dockyard Church
16. Officers' Stables
17. Sail Loft
18. Commissioner's House
19. Commissioner's Office
20. Officers' Terrace
21. Main Offices
22. Present Use Store
23. Dock Pumping Station
24. Smithery
25. House Carpenters' Shop
26. Timber Seasoning Sheds
27. Mast Houses
28. Mast Houses and Mould
    Loft
29. Sawmills
30. South Mast Pond
31. North Mast Pond
32. Boat store
33. Guardhouse
34. No. 3 Slip
35. No. 4 Slip
36. No. 5 Slip
37. No. 6 Slip
38. No. 7 Slip
39. Area of land reclaimed
    1835–50
Buildings in outline no longer
  survive, except for 34–38
Stippled areas are for timber
  storage

Fig. 4. Chatham Dockyard
c. 1850.

0		100		200		300 metres
0	100		500			1000 feet

by the dockyard craftsmen but the rest by a contractor (9, 83). Where building contracts survive, the frugal Navy Board usually stipulated that it would
provide any timber required, a sensible arrangement as it already monopolised the English timber market and frequently had suitable second-hand
timber from ships or buildings being taken apart. There is no evidence,
despite persistent legends to the contrary, that prisoner of war labour was
used to construct buildings. Quite apart from the problems of supervision,
the Navy Board was far too frightened of arson. Only in the nineteenth
century were ordinary prisoners used, in chain gangs, for manual labour.

10. *Opposite below* The
southern end of Chatham
Dockyard in 1774, showing
a medley of storehouses on
Anchor Wharf with the
long timber buildings of the
ropery beyond. This area
was to be extensively
rebuilt between 1780 and
1805.

11. *Right* Portsmouth
Dockyard firemen c. 1900.
Behind them is the 1840's
cast iron water tower. This
replaced a timber one
erected in the 1790s when a
fire fighting main was installed in the yard and
sprinklers were proposed
for some of the buildings.
The tower still remains
although the water tank has
long gone.

12. *Right* Portsmouth
Dockyard. This, the first
steam engine to be used by
the navy, was installed in
1797. Designed by Sadler,
the mechanic on Bentham's
staff, it pumped docks at
night and powered wood-
working machinery by day.
Its site can still be seen
inside the blockmills.

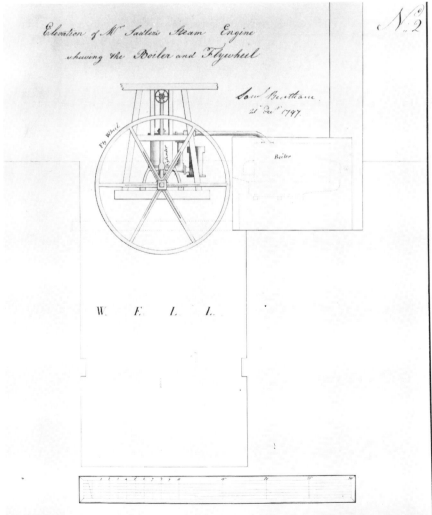

At the overseas bases problems multiplied, and it is one of the greatest of unrecorded naval achievements that so many of these were overcome before modern communications shrank the world. Distance was the first obstacle, with correspondence taking months. At most of the bases except Gibraltar and Malta, workmen were in perennially short supply and very high wages were necessary to tempt labour to forsake comparatively healthy England for the frequently fatal warmer climes. Materials were another problem and no Mediterranean, Atlantic or Caribbean base had a hinterland that enabled it to be self-sufficient from the start in all building materials.

13. *Top* Chatham Dockyard c. 1804. The great majority of the buildings shown here still survive, making Chatham the last relatively intact example of a Georgian Dockyard. This painting by Pocock hangs in the National Maritime Museum.

14. *Opposite* Minorca, Port Mahon naval base in the early eighteenth century. The majority of the buildings are storehouses.

The Navy Board in London and individual officers overseas were to employ diverse methods to overcome these various difficulties. Soon after the capture of Minorca, ships' crews were busy constructing wharves and careening areas and when London proved tardy in providing money for a hospital (**144**) the officers dipped into their own pockets to fund the project. It took the unfortunate Admiral Jennings at least eighteen months and a petition to Queen Anne to recover sums owed to him and his subordinates.

To the end of its existence in 1832 the Navy Board was never able to exert close control over building activities at foreign yards and this problem remained insurmountable with slow and uncertain communications and local officers adept at interpreting instructions fairly liberally. It should not be forgotten too that the Navy Board was having to learn by experience; it had no precedents to which it could turn for an answer. But as it grew in experience it began to tame some of the logistics. A combination of merchant ships, naval transports and warships kept yards supplied. Where materials could be obtained locally, they were, although this was not always straightforward: in 1799 an enterprising contractor building a reservoir at Gibraltar tried to obtain bricks from nearby Spain by using vessels flying Moorish colours. This ingenious ploy failed and nearly a million bricks had to be shipped from England instead.

On the whole, Mediterranean bases presented the fewest problems, although they all lacked timber. But in the West Indies, almost everything

15. Gibraltar Dockyard in the late 1880s. Until extensive additions at the very end of the nineteenth century, Gibraltar remained comparatively unimportant, eclipsed first by Minorca and then by Malta. The dockyard buildings can be seen in the middle distance beyond the bastioned defences.

Fig. 5. Devonport Dockyard c. 1850.

had to be imported and labour was scarce. Here, prefabrication was a solution adopted remarkably early. Large timber-framed buildings, some a hundred feet long, came out in sections from England in the late 1720s to Port Antonio and English Harbour. By the 1740s the system was sufficiently organised for yard officers in Antigua to state their needs to the Navy Board in London and for the latter to have buildings constructed in North America for freighting south in sections. Armies of wood-boring ants finally put paid to this remarkable traffic and more durable buildings were constructed, brick, tiles and slates voyaging from the Thames to the Caribbean either as ballast in warships or in Navy Board transports. Later, cast iron revived the possibilities of prefabrication and in 1817 a complete two-storey hospital 400 feet long was largely built of this material shipped in sections to Port Royal, Jamaica, where it still stands, surviving even the great earthquake of 1907. At Ireland Island, Bermuda, the commissioner's magnificently sited house arrived in transports throughout the 1820s, and although Holl and later Taylor hoped that this would enable them to keep an eye on the quality of materials and the cost, they reckoned without

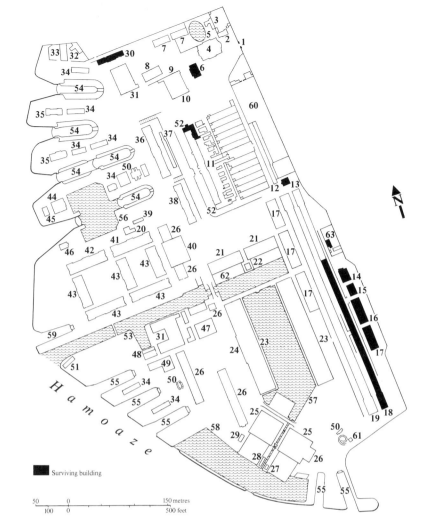

Key:

1. Main Gate
2. Master Warden's House
3. Stables
4. Chapel
5. Reservoir
6. Pay Office
7. Team stables
8. Painters' Shed.
9. Painters' Workshop.
10. Guardhouse.
11. Officers' Terrace.
12. Officers' Stables
13. Master Ropemaker's Offices
14. White Yarn Houses
15. Tarring House
16. Black Yarn House
17. Hemp Houses
18. Spinning House
19. Laying House
20. Topping House
21. Boathouse
22. Office
23. Plank Store with Mast Locks underneath
24. Mould Loft
25. Masthouses
26. Sawpits
27. Cabin
28. Hemp and Pitch House
29. Guardhouse
30. Plumbers' Shop
31. Smithery
32. Bricklayers' Yard
33. House Carpenters' Workshop
34. Shipwrights' Sheds
35. Dry-docks' pump
36. Joiners' Workshop
37. Sheds
38. Main Offices
39. Cabin
40. Timber Yard
41. Rigging House
42. Sail Loft
43. Quadrangle Storehouses
44. Offices
45. Cabin
46. Cabin
47. Carpenters' Workshop
48. Stores
49. Stores
50. Steaming Kilns
51. Offices
52. The original 1692 Offices
53. South Channel
54. Dry-docks
55. Building Slips
56. 1692 Wet-Dock
57. Inner Mast Pond
58. Outer Mast Pond
59. Graving Slip
60. Former Commissioner's Garden
61. Gazebo
62. Boat Pond
63. Master Ropemaker's House

■ Surviving building

Bermuda labour costs and the building ambitions of commissioners on the other side of the Atlantic. Nobody ever did find out how much money was spent on this project (112).

Financing all these royal dockyards was a perpetual headache. During peacetime governments resented the costs and applied economies wherever possible: during wartime results of these same economies frequently led to criticism, often from the same government ministers. Dockyard planning was rarely anything other than piecemeal, although there are notable exceptions with Portsmouth and Plymouth in the 1760s and 1780s. The victualling yards existed in the same hand to mouth atmosphere until the 1820s when the Royal Clarence Yard at Gosport and the superb Royal William Yard at Stonehouse were constructed. Later the steam-driven all-metal warships caused a revolution in dockyard facilities, and huge sums were expended from the 1840s to 1870s, creating in effect new dockyards grafted on to the old.

In many ways the middle of the eighteenth century was the most testing time for the Navy Board and dockyard officials. Warships were growing

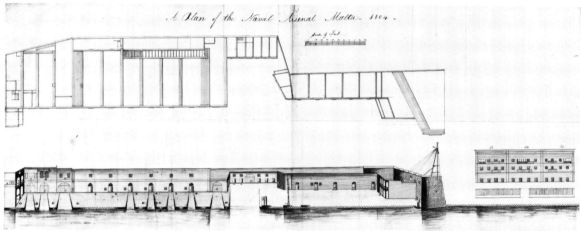

16. *Top* Malta. The for-
mer dockyard in 1972. In
the distance is the first dry-
dock to be successfully
completed in an overseas
base. It dates from the
1840s. To the right are the
galley arches shown in
plate 17. The arcaded top is
a short-lived ropery added
early on by the Royal Navy.

17. *Above* Malta Dockyard
in 1804. A survey showing
the casemated storehouses
and sheerlegs inherited
from the Knights.
Surrounding defences made
Malta one of the most
strongly defended of all
naval bases.

34

18. Antigua Dockyard, now perhaps the most idyllic of all overseas bases. Its small scale is immediately apparent. Abandoned by the Royal Navy in 1889, it has been the subject of a careful restoration programme over the last 30 years.

ever larger, making existing docks and ships obsolete, the fleet as a whole was increasing year by year, voyages were becoming longer and a series of wars kept yards fully stretched as well as exposing their deficiencies. By the end of the Seven Years War it was clear that drastic expansion and modernisation was needed at the three main home bases of Chatham, Portsmouth and Plymouth. For the next 40 years the latter two yards were extensively reconstructed and when work here was tailing off, money was found for a more piecemeal modernisation of Chatham. The work done then was to stand the Royal Navy in good stead during the long years of war with Revolutionary and Napoleonic France and many of the buildings and engineering works constructed then still remain in use today (4, 13).

Towards the end of the eighteenth century the Navy Board was frequently criticised for not being more receptive to technological developments. One result, already noted, was the appointment by the Admiralty of Bentham and his small department in 1795. In the Navy Board's defence, the steam engines of the day were very inefficient and expensive and until

19. *Opposite top* Port Royal, Jamaica, in 1897. This sleepy outpost of empire was to be closed soon after this photograph was taken. As at Antigua, most of the buildings were for stores of one sort or another. Beyond, symbol of Victorian *Pax Britannia*, lies the guard ship.

20. *Opposite bottom* HMS *Achilles* nears completion at Chatham in 1863. The first iron armour-plated warship to be built in a government dockyard anywhere in the world was laid down following the success of HMS *Warrior*. These ships inaugurated not just a naval revolution but also a dockyard revolution, leading to expansion programmes to accommodate the machine shops, boiler shops and larger dry-docks now necessary.

21. *Right* Malta. The new factory nearing completion in 1887, typical of many such metal-working shops erected in the main bases between 1860 and c. 1900.

22. *Below right* Expansion of Portsmouth Dockyard c. 1901. Such scenes were familiar at Chatham, Devonport, Malta and Gibraltar as the Admiralty invested huge sums to update its most important bases.

repetitive processes using machine tools were developed their economic dockyard uses were strictly limited. Dock pumping was an obvious application but this was an intermittent process and the horse gins then in use, although slow, had the merit that their motive power could be used elsewhere in the dockyard when not required in the gins. The roperies were another possibility, but it is doubtful if before the nineteenth century there existed an engine powerful enough, while the Navy Board had a very justifiable fear of fire in these. Portsmouth ropery was burnt down three times between 1760 and 1776 and part of Plymouth Dock ropeyard suffered a

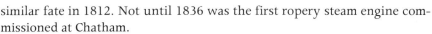

similar fate in 1812. Not until 1836 was the first ropery steam engine commissioned at Chatham.

Bentham himself was not an outstanding inventor, although he had some success with various power-driven woodworking machines. His real strength lay in recognising possibilities when he saw them and he struck lucky with Marc Isambard Brunel. Brunel's machines for making ships' blocks were an outstanding success, the first ever use of machine tools for mass-production. The building put up for them at Portsmouth in 1802 still survives along with complete sets of machine tools, in use until recently (**74, 75, 76**). At Chatham they collaborated again by 1812 with an ambitious steam-driven sawmill incorporating an overhead railway. After teething troubles this too was an unqualified success and although no longer in use, the building remains (**77**).

The blockmills and the sawmills were pioneering efforts, gaining the dockyards experience with steam engines years before a reluctant Admiralty sanctioned a steam-powered vessel. Indeed, for a few years in the early nineteenth century the royal dockyards could be said to be in the van of technical progress. Later, as steam engines became more reliable and powerful, new uses were found for them and by the 1850s boiler house chimneys punctuated the skylines of all the home yards and several of those overeas (**24**).

Fear of fire, whether accident or arson, made the Navy Board very receptive to fireproofing schemes. Replacing timber buildings with brick and stone was one method, consciously adopted from the 1760s onwards when finance permitted. Thin iron plates nailed to the undersides of floor joists and boards was another less happy expedient tried in the 1780s, but it was not until cast and wrought iron became available as a substitute for timber that really fireproof buildings could be constructed. Probably the earliest is the curious little pay office in Portsmouth (**89**), but the most ambitious early application was the reconstruction of the 1200-feet-long east ropery at Plymouth Dock after the 1812 fire (**66**). Shortly before then, as part of the same process, fire mains were proposed and installed in the main dockyards and a project to put sprinklers inside buildings was also mooted. Alongside this use of new materials went development of the old, nowhere more striking than in the vast and graceful timber roofs over building slips and dry-docks (**36**).

The change from sail to steam for propulsion and from wood to metal for construction had profound effects on the royal dockyards. Not only were the new warships of the 1860s larger than their predecessors, but they demanded a whole new technology to build and maintain them. Foundries and machine shops superseded sawmills and sail lofts; the scale changed and the pace quickened. If it did nothing else, the all-metal warship ushered in the age of accelerating obsolescence.

To cope with this upheaval while maintaining the existing if largely outdated fleet the Admiralty grafted what amounted to new dockyards on to the main existing ones. Woolwich proved too cramped for such sur-

23. *Previous page, top* The north end of Portsmouth Dockyard about 75 years ago. All the dry-docks in the foreground were planned at the end of Victoria's reign. The rural aspect north of the harbour is a remarkable contrast to today's urban sprawl.

24. *Previous page, bottom* Portsmouth. An early twentieth-century view of the Steam Basin, now No. 2 Basin, begun in 1843 for the new steam-powered warships. On the far side is the contemporary 2 Ship Shop and beyond it No. 1 Smithery of 1852 with its five chimneys. Beyond the latter are the roofs of the cast-iron slip housings, constructed in the 1840s just ahead of the still extant set at Chatham. To the right of the top of the tall chimney to the left are the 1802 Block Mills. The vast difference in scale between Georgian and Victorian dockyard architecture is at once apparent.

25. *Top right* Portsmouth Dockyard coaling point in 1908. From the 1850s until the navy changed to oil-fired boilers, such coaling points were prominent, vital and unpopular features of every naval base.

26. *Above right* Bermuda victualling yard was built as part of the mid-nineteenth-century expansion of this Atlantic base. In the foreground are store-keepers' houses.

gery and was closed, but Portsmouth, Chatham, Devonport and Malta all had sizeable additions from the 1840s to 1860s. Later Bermuda and Gibraltar were to be modernised and extended. Lesser dockyards, particularly those overseas, had to be content with perhaps a coaling jetty and an extended smithery to cope with bunkering and emergency repairs. Some failed to survive long in this new age: Antigua Dockyard closed in 1889 and was replaced by a Fortified Coaling Station at Castries, St Lucia; Port Royal closed in 1907. Others followed as the Royal Navy relinquished its global role.

Today, Britain's naval history is studded with the names of famous men, great sea battles and epic voyages. But behind all these, and making them possible, were the royal dockyards. In them are preserved in the form of architecture and engineering works tangible links with Great Britain's proud naval tradition, while within the present confines of Chatham naval base, to be closed in 1984, is a virtually complete and now unique Georgian dockyard (13).

Chapter 2

Building and Maintaining the Fleet

The size of the fleet and its individual warships determined the scale and number of shore bases. Although there were inevitable fluctuations between periods of peace and war, for more than two centuries after 1700 the underlying trend was towards an expanding navy. Not only were there more warships; the warships themselves were becoming larger. At the beginning of the eighteenth century a first-rate of 90 guns displaced under 1,500 tons; a century later, third-rates of nearly 2,000 tons were common. When metal warships were introduced in the second half of the nineteenth century their lengths and displacements were beyond the wildest dreams of Georgian shipwrights. Only with the recent disappearance of the great battleships and aircraft carriers have British capital ship sizes started to reduce, but even now a modern frigate dwarfs HMS *Victory*, emphasising just how comparatively small were warships of the sailing navy and how extraordinary were their achievements and those of their crews.

The effect of a growing fleet in the eighteenth century resulted in creation of new dockyards and expansion of existing facilities directly concerned with shipbuilding and repairing. While merchant yards built most of the navy's smaller warships, the largest ones, the first- and second-rates, were generally the prerogative of the royal dockyards, which also had to maintain the fleet as a whole.

The actual construction of wooden warships could involve little in the way of expensive capital equipment with the result that there are few tangible remains associated directly with warship building before the nineteenth century. Although eighteenth-century master shipwrights liked to build warships in dry-docks to avoid launching problems, this was wasteful use of an expensive asset specifically designed for ship repair, and the great majority of warships were built on slips. Such slips were usually of wooden construction and had a comparatively short life, while those which survived the weakening effects of wet rot found themselves obsolete as warship sizes increased. Later in the eighteenth century brick and stone were used for slip construction, but although more durable slips resulted they were no more immune to obsolescence. Only one eighteenth-century slip remains today; this is No 1 slip at Devonport built in 1774–5 and for long equipped with launching cradles enabling it to be used for repairing small craft. Its timber roof is an early nineteenth-century addition, smallest of the three surviving timber slip roofs (36).

In a royal dockyard the method of building wooden warships changed

little. Once the master shipwright had completed his designs the cross sections were drawn out full-size on the flat wooden floor of a mould loft. Templates were then made from thin fir scantlings and these were taken to the shipwrights at the building slip. Mould floors had to be large and uninterrupted by structural supports, a requirement most easily met in cramped and busy dockyards by placing them at the top of buildings where there were no higher floors needing supporting pillars—hence the term *mould loft*. Like slips, they had to be enlarged to keep pace with warship sizes, and the three eighteenth-century ones which remain owe their survival to their adaptability as storehouses and offices. Part of the present 24 Storehouse at Portsmouth, built in 1790, was once a mould loft, as was the 1722 Clocktower building at Chatham (**82**). But historically the most important one, also at Chatham, is the combined masthouse and mould loft begun in 1753. A few years after is completion the huge mould floor— 55 feet wide and 120 feet long—was almost certainly used to lay out the lines of HMS *Victory*. Very probably her original masts and spars were fashioned on the ground floor and this large timber-framed building along with the former sail loft are the last direct links at Chatham with Nelson's famous flagship (**29**). The mould loft continued in use until late in the nineteenth century, towards the end of its life being used for the lines of HMS *Achilles*, the first armour-plated all-metal warship to be built in a government dockyard anywhere in the world (**20**). By then, warships' sizes were such that much larger floors had become necessary, a problem overcome at Devonport where one of the covered slips was floored over as a mould floor or screive board, to give it the name used when building metal ships.

Until the beginning of the nineteenth century a warship's timber was

27. *Opposite top* The only eighteenth-century slip remaining in a royal dockyard. This was built at Plymouth in the 1770s; the timber roof was added forty years later.

28. *Opposite bottom* A ship on the stocks at Deptford by John Clevely, painted in the 1770s. In the foreground is a timber-lined dry dock. Such docks, cheap to construct, were very expensive to maintain. Some survived at Chatham into the nineteenth century, although the first stone dry-docks with stepped sides had come into use at Portsmouth and Plymouth in the 1690s.

29. *Right* Chatham Dockyard. The mast houses and mould loft begun in 1753. HMS *Victory*'s lines were almost certainly laid out here and her first masts made on the ground floor.

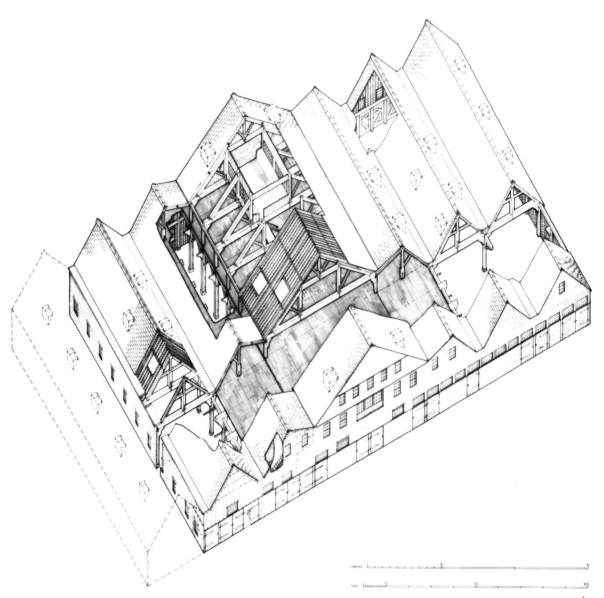

30. Chatham Dockyard. Axonometric view of the mast houses and mould loft showing the sturdy timber construction and the mould floor, a clear space 120 × 55 feet, where the cross sections of warships were drawn out full size so that templates could be formed for the shipwrights.

pit sawn, a laborious and labour intensive process which has left few traces. Sawpits were usually grouped together, often covered with a simple tiled roof. Only where they were incorporated into more substantial buildings does evidence for them survive. The northern end of the Chatham Clock-tower building once had such a group while a longer range, dating from just after the Napoleonic war, remains at Sheerness (33). The only complete one is in Antigua dockyard, its small size indicative of occasional use when warships needed repairs (32).

The application of steam power to sawing promised enormous savings in manpower and it was one of Bentham's interests in the late 1790s, but not until Marc Brunel produced designs for large-scale mechanical sawmills in 1811 was anything done. Chatham, as a shipbuilding yard, was chosen for one of the sawmills which began operation in 1814. The Chatham saw-mill, which still exists, was for its time breathtakingly daring in concept. Logs for the mill, which stood on higher ground to the east of the dockyard, were floated along an underground canal tunnel from the south mast pond to an elliptical vertical shaft adjacent to the mill. Timbers up to 70 feet long came to the surface on a cradle raised by a counterbalance tank fed by condensor water from the steam engine. They were then picked up by a crane running on an overhead railway and stacked on either side of the track. The same crane, powered by a chain from the sawmill engine, retrieved logs as required and fed them to the sawframes (77).

In exceptional circumstances a warship could be building for a decade, its incomplete hull exposed to all weathers and highly vulnerable to rot even before the vessel was launched. The rot was aggravated by use of green timbers, largely the fault of government parsimony in peacetime. When shipbuilding programmes were accelerated at the outbreak of war it was rare for dockyards to have in stock reserves of seasoned timber. So serious was this problem in the Seven Years War (1756–63) that it consti-tuted a greater danger to the longevity of naval warships than ever the French did. One result was a determination by the Admiralty to ensure reserves of good timber and to further this laudable aim very large quanti-ties of timber seasoning sheds were built in all the home dockyards in

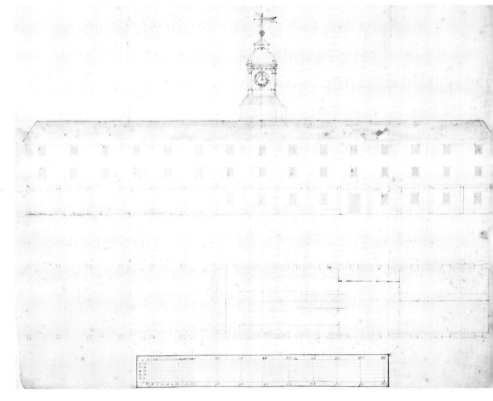

31. Chatham Dockyard. The 1723 storehouse which incorporates sawpits at one end of the ground floor. The two upper floors, orig-inally timber-framed, were rebuilt in brick in 1803. This is the oldest surviving dockyard storehouse (see plate 82).

the 1770s. In essence these were stoutly constructed timber-framed sheds protected by tiled roofs with louvred gables and sides to promote air circulation. Inside were tiers of strong wooden racks on which the sawn timber was stacked. Although an architecturally humble class of dockyard building, they were vital to the durability of the late Georgian and early Victorian fleet, but today only two survive, both at Chatham (35).

The next stage was to build warships under cover, but technical problems and costs of constructing the huge roofs necessary to protect 100-gun ships on the stocks were such that no attempt seems to have been made before the nineteenth century. Bentham first interested himself in the problem in 1807, visiting the Swedish naval base at Karlskrona to see covered slips there. It was almost certainly the result of his initiative that such structures were erected in the home dockyards a few years later. Portsmouth had roofs over some of its slips and dry-docks by 1814 and Chatham followed within three years. In 1817 the Board of Admiralty reported unequivocally in their favour with the result that none of the home dockyards lacked these graceful structures which in sheer size dwarfed everything around them.

Covering a slip at that time stretched timber technology virtually to its limits, but its properties were well understood by the yard shipwrights who undoubtedly contributed their experience and skills to the design and construction. Compound timber pillars supported the roofs which were steeply pitched to gain extra height and were cantilevered over the actual slips. Many had apsidal ends to protect the bows of ships below. A variety of roofing materials were tried including tarred paper and slates, but copper or zinc sheets were eventually preferred and the former must have shone and glowed until dulled and greened by the weather. Some housings were over 300 feet long, clear spanning slips up to 60 feet wide. Dry-docks not required for masted ships were likewise given roofs but these did not need to be quite as tall, for vessels obviously sat much lower in docks.

By the early 1840s iron technology had advanced to a stage where it was possible to design all-metal slip housings, using cast and wrought iron for the frames and cladding the structures in the recently invented corrugated iron sheets. Portsmouth was modernising some of its slips then so it was the first dockyard to have such housings, two of which were built in 1844. Chatham was likewise laying out new slips near the northern end of the then dockyard and three of the new housings were built here in 1847–8. These differed in detail from those at Portsmouth and were significantly better braced, but both groups had elegantly curved main trusses over the slips. Three years after completion of the Chatham set, Colonel Green of the Royal Engineers designed a further slip housing which was added to the northern end of the Medway group. Its sturdy, well-braced frame makes it barely distinguishable from later metal-framed structures such as large factories and aircraft hangars, and with its completion large-scale metal-framing may be said to have come of age (38, 39).

Portsmouth, Chatham, Deptford and Woolwich seem to have been alone

Fig. 6. Antigua Dockyard c. 1800. A fairly typical example of a smaller overseas base.

Key:
1. Main Gate and Guardhouse
2. Storehouse
3. Boathouse; Sail Loft over
4. Boathouse; Joiners' Workshop over
5. Sawpits
6. Smiths' Shop
7. Working Masthouses; Stores over
8. Storehouse
9. Kitchen for crews of ships on careen
10. Capstan House
11. Careening Wharf
12. Storehouse
13. Master Shipwright's House
14. Master Shipwright's kitchen and storeroom
15. Careening Wharf
16. East Capstan House
17. Kitchen for crews of ships on careen
18. Pursers' Provisions Storeroom and Storeroom for Ships' small arms when careening.
19. Storehouse for careening gear
20. Storehouse
21. Commander in Chief's House

Antigua Dockyard

St. Helena

11
10
9
8
7
3
2
3
4
21
5
13
14
12
1
6

17
18
15
16
19
20

N

0   30   60 metres
0   100   200 feet

Harbour mouth

Same scale

Falmouth

Falmouth
Harbour

English
Harbour
Town

Ordnance
Bay

Tank
Bay

SEE ABOVE

Freemans
Bay

English Harbour

t above sea level

400 and over
300
200
100 feet

0   200   400   600   800 metres
0   1000 2000 3000 feet

in having metal slip housings, for within a few years of their completion all-metal warships were being built, which did not need such elaborate protection when under construction. Over the years, housings were demolished or destroyed by fire and today only three timber ones remain: two at Devonport and one at Chatham. The Chatham example, which dates from 1838, forms the southern end of a remarkable group, for the other four housings here are the three 1847–8 and the 1852 metal slips. This group of metal housings, although comparatively unknown, predates the great metal train sheds at Kings Cross and Paddington which are usually cited as pioneers in wide-span coverings. Further north in Chatham dockyard is another small group of metal slip housings, first erected at Woolwich dockyard and then when that yard closed in 1869 transferred to Chatham and adapted as machine shops.

The most expensive installations connected with shipbuilding and especially with repairing, and ones which were crucial in determining the exact location of a dockyard were the docks themselves. These took two forms: dry-docks and wet-docks, the significant difference being that the latter were not designed to be pumped dry. Their purpose was to provide sheltered wharfage and a constant level of water irrespective of tidal fluctuations. A constant level greatly simplified the securing of ships and also made working on them that much easier. In their late seventeenth-century form they were comparatively small stone-lined basins with double sets of inward and outward opening gates linking with the tidal areas. Warships entered at high tide, the gates were shut and this high tide level was then maintained in the basin. Except for the gates there were no mechanical parts, but considerable engineering skills were nevertheless needed for the basin walls had to be particularly strong to resist pressure from storms and the differing levels of water within and without, and failures early on were fairly common.

32. Antigua Dockyard. These two sawpits sufficed for this small overseas base, in contrast to the batteries of pits in the major shipbuilding dockyards. Not until 1814 was mechanical sawing on a large scale first introduced at Chatham.

33. Sheerness Dockyard. The long building constructed in the 1820s had sawpits and plank racks on the ground floor with a mould floor and joiners shop overhead.

Not all the home dockyards had wet-docks, or basins as they became known in the nineteenth century. The oldest, late seventeenth-century in part, is No 1 Basin at Portsmouth into which HMS *Victory*'s dry-dock once opened (**41**). This basin remains as finally completed, after several extensions, in 1805. Its small scale contrasts with the much larger No 2 Basin laid out to the north in the 1840s for the new steam-propelled warships (**79**). Chatham managed without a wet-dock until the 1860s when St Mary's Creek was enlarged, given locks and turned into the largest set of basins owned by the Royal Navy. Abroad, the navy managed without such luxuries. The Mediterranean, largely tideless, had no real need of them while the Caribbean bases were too unimportant and like Bermuda were not expected to carry out major overhauls or to lay-up warships.

Dry-docks, as their name implies, were intended to be drained dry, either by gravity or by pumping, so that shipwrights could work on the hull of a vessel. The first dry-dock was constructed at Portsmouth in 1495 on the orders of Henry VII and was a comparatively crude affair. It relied on gravity drainage at low tide and its staggered timber gates overlapped so that the space between could be filled with clay and stones to make a waterproof seal. Docking and undocking were clearly long-drawn-out processes and not ones lightly undertaken. Nevertheless, Henry's dock contained all the essential elements of later dry-docks but its expense was such that not all dockyards had one from the start—Chatham, founded in 1547, made shift without until the 1620s.

Successive generations of shipwrights and civil engineers strove to improve dry-docks and their efforts were concentrated on three particular aspects: the actual construction material, the dock gates and methods of drainage. By the end of the eighteenth century they had mastered most of the problems and thereafter dry-docks grew larger and more efficient by evolutionary rather than revolutionary stages.

34. *Top right* Chatham
Dockyard. Part of the 1774
model showing timber sea-
soning sheds. Such were
erected in large numbers in
the 1770s to try to ensure
adequate supplies of sea-
soned timber and to lessen
the crippling incidence of
rot in new warships.

35. *Above right* Chatham
Dockyard. This base pos-
sesses the only two eigh-
teenth-century seasoning
sheds. Such architecturally
humble structures played a
major part in producing a
more durable fleet during
the Napoleonic wars.
This range has recently
been restored.

Like wet-docks, dry-docks had to be strongly built to resist pressure, especially when empty. Then, particularly in the soft soil of Portsea Island or the banks of the Medway, there was always a danger of collapse brought about either by water or soil pressure. However, not until Edward Dummer laid out Plymouth Dock in the 1690s and modernised Portsmouth (**40**) was anything stronger than timber used to line dry-docks. Dummer used stone, enabling him to step the insides of dry-docks for the first time, but the expense of stone was such that the Thames and Medway yards continued to use timber for a further century in spite of its high maintenance costs.

Dock gates were more of a problem for it was their width and the depth of water over the cill that largely determined the maximum size of warship able to use a particular dry-dock. As warships grew larger, a dry-dock could be lengthened without major problems, but widening and especially deepening it was tantamount to building a complete new installation.

By the end of the seventeenth century, dock gates had improved in de-sign from the overlapping ones of 1495 at Portsmouth and were now formed of three hinged leaves but these still required up to 70 men to operate them. When Edward Dummer was building his stone dry-dock at Plymouth (**3**) he installed and possibly invented the modern type of twin gates, angled outwards to better resist water pressure when the dock was empty. He claimed that only four to six men were needed to work them. Each gate had a vertical sluicegate to speed refilling, but in the eighteenth century

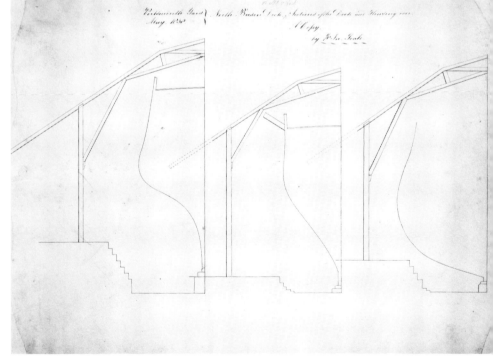

36. *Above* Devonport
Dockyard. The 1770s' slip
with its later timber roof.
This dockyard roofed its
docks and slips between
1815 and 1821. This is the
smallest of the three surviving timber roofs and is the
only one over a slip still in
use. To the right is the
imposing figurehead of
HMS *Royal William*, a
120-gun first-rate of 1833.

37. *Right* Portsmouth
Dockyard. A drawing of
1838 showing sections of a
proposed timber roof. The
scale is apparent from the
profiles of the warship.

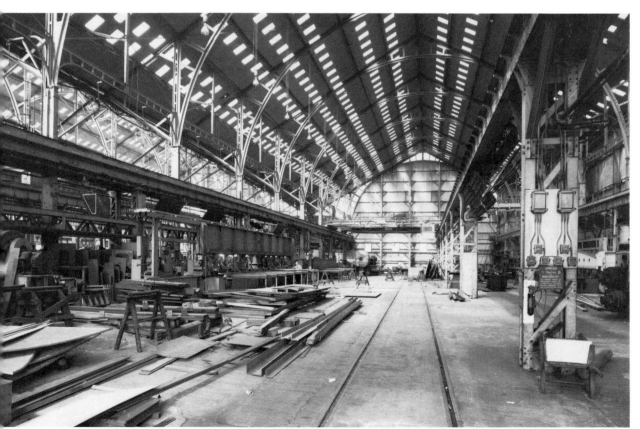

38. *Left* Chatham Dock-yard's unique range of covered slips. From right to left, 3 slip and its all-timber roof of 1838, 4–6 slips with metal roofs of 1847 and 7 slip with its metal roof completed in 1855. All were designed to protect wooden warships. 7 slip remained in use until 1966, used almost exclusively this century to build submarines.

39. *Bottom left* Portsmouth Dockyard. The interior of the pioneer metal slip roofs before demolition in 1979. The 1847 examples at Chatham are almost identical.

these were replaced by culverts as the sluices were found to leak and to weaken the gates.

A century after Dummer, Bentham was responsible for the next major technical advance in dry-dock construction. Until late in the eighteenth century floors of docks continued to be built of heavy timbers or brick largely independent of the stone sides. This was apt to cause structural problems, especially with soft subsoil, and any subsidence almost invariably led to difficulties with the fit of the gates. Bentham sought to solve this by tying the gate piers firmly together by an inverted masonry arch under the cill. Although correspondence is not clear, it seems that the present No 3 Dock at Portsmouth started in 1799 was the first to use this principle and that the inverted arch was extended the full length of the dry-dock effectively linking both sides. Variations of this became standard for most subsequent dry-docks.

Bentham's second contribution was the re-invention of the caisson, the principles of which first seem to have been advocated by Commissioner St Lo at Chatham in 1703. A caisson had several advantages: there were no troublesome hinges, it was constructed as one unit thus lessening potential leaks at joints, and its broad top could be used as a roadway. The last was a considerable advantage and in some dockyards, notably at No 1 Basin at Portsmouth, it saved long detours.

Early dry-docks were comparatively shallow and could be drained at low tide by gravity, but this simple method became impossible as depths increased to match larger warships. By the eighteenth century deeper docks were drained by horse-driven chain pumps, a slow and inefficient method which could lead to tiresome delays in moving warships after refit. In 1764 the dockyard officers at Portsmouth proposed an ingenious solution which remains in use there to this day. They deepened Dummer's North Basin of 1690 and turned it into a vast sump linked by culverts and sluices to the adjacent dry-docks. The latter could then drain quickly by gravity into the former North Basin and the water be pumped from it at leisure by chain pumps. This work was put in hand in 1771 and in 1797 chain pumps were replaced here by a steam pump, the first instance of use of a steam engine in a royal dockyard. Shortly afterwards, the old North Basin was covered by two tiers of vaults; the following century electric pumps replaced steam, but vaults, basin and culverts remain as completed.

Steam pumping was a considerable improvement and was introduced at Chatham in the second decade of the nineteenth century when its dry-docks were rebuilt; there the engine house remains as does the pioneer one at Portsmouth, which now is part of the blockmills (**74**).

Double docks, where a second ship could be secured astern of the first, enjoyed a popularity early on where waterfront space was limited. However, the need to co-ordinate repair programmes on the ships using them made for inefficiency and by the early nineteenth century none remained (**42**). Curiously, the first overseas yard to propose a dry-dock advocated

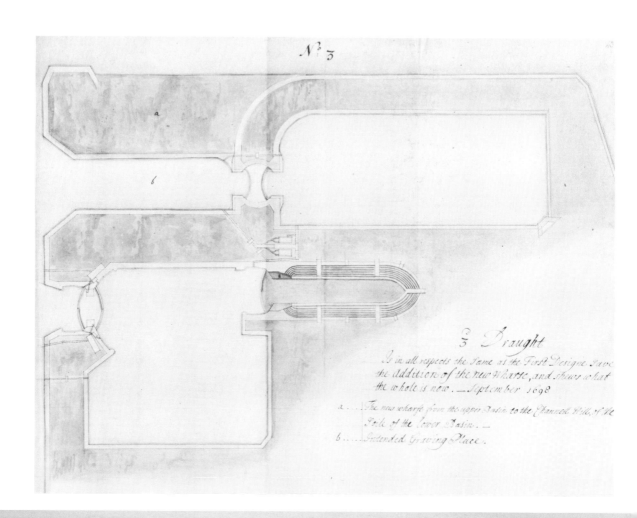

N.º 3

3 Draught

Is in all respects the same as the First Designe save the addition of the new wharfe, and shews what the whole is now. — September 1698

a ..... The new wharfe from the upper Basin to the Channell side of the Soile of the lower Basin. —

b ..... Intended Graving Place.

40. *Opposite top* Portsmouth Dockyard. Dummer's pioneer scheme of 1690 for a stone-stepped dry-dock and two wet-docks, similar to his contemporary design for Plymouth. Here at Portsmouth he had to install chain pumps. The upper wet-dock still remains below the Block Mills, now used as a giant sump for draining the adjacent dry-docks.

41. *Opposite bottom* Portsmouth Dockyard. No. 1 Basin and dry-docks. Part of the basin dates from the 1690s, but the dry-docks are all Georgian, the last completed in 1805. This is the only eighteenth-century group remaining.

42. *Right* Plymouth Dockyard. Part of the 1774 model showing a double dock. Such docks enjoyed popularity in the seventeenth and eighteenth centuries where space at wharves was limited, but the inconveniences of having to synchronise repair times on both ships gradually led to their abandonment.

a double one, the last time any yard favoured such. This was English Harbour, Antigua, in 1795, but it differed significantly from other designs for it was planned to construct it across a short neck of land and to give it gates at both ends.

At home, Chatham had the largest number of dry-docks by the end of the seventeenth century—four single and a double—but thereafter it was eclipsed by the south-coast yards until the 1860s. Overseas, Malta followed Antigua in proposing a dry-dock in 1806 and construction actually started in 1811, but faults in the bedrock proved so serious that the project was abandoned a few years later and it was not until the 1840s that Malta became the first overseas base to acquire a dry-dock (**16**). Bermuda suffered from the same problem of porous and fissured rock that had caused such difficulties at Malta and in 1818, the year that the first Malta dry-dock project was abandoned, Rennie proposed a novel solution for Bermuda. He suggested that a hole for a dry-dock should be excavated and an iron lining be fabricated in England and shipped out. 40 years later, one of the first iron floating-docks was sent to these islands.

Much of the mid-nineteenth-century modernisation of the dockyards concentrated on the provision of new basins and dry-docks at the major bases; these are seen to best advantage at Chatham which has the largest

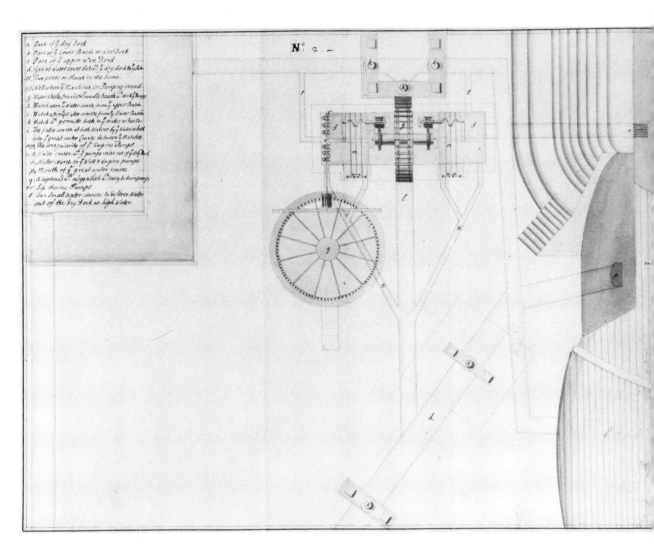

43. *Opposite top* Chatham Dockyard. The huge basins formed in the 1860s from St Mary's Creek. These are the largest such mid-Victorian engineering works and contrast with the scale of Georgian civil engineering (plate 41). The locks in the foreground lead to the Medway, while machine shops and foundries lie in the upper centre of this view. To the left are the ordered ranks of Pembroke Naval Barracks constructed at the beginning of this century. An aerial view taken in May 1982 shortly before the transfer of Chatham-based warships to Portsmouth, Devonport and the breakers' yards.

44. *Opposite bottom* Portsmouth Dockyard. No. 1 dock, still substantially as completed at the end of the eighteenth century. Prominent are the stone aulters or steps and the chutes for sliding materials to the bottom. Beyond is HMS *Victory*.

45. *Above* Portsmouth Dockyard. Part of Dummer's elaborate design for dock pumping in the 1690s. A horse gin was connected to a series of chain pumps which were also to be driven by a water-wheel. The latter could only work at low tide when it was fed by a culvert from the wet dock. It is not known if this scheme was every fully implemented. Hitherto, chain pumps had been manually worked.

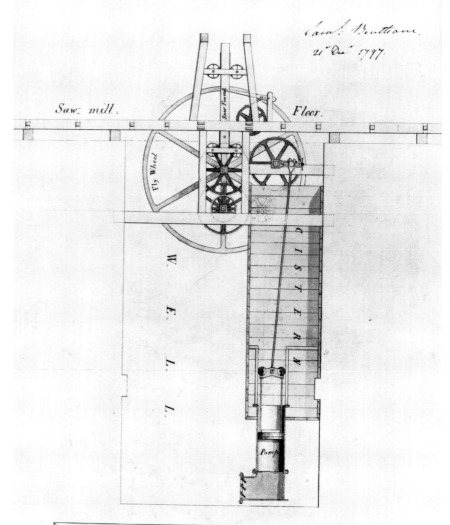

Section of the Pumping & Sawing Apparatus Nᵒ 3

Saml Bentham
21ˢᵗ Decʳ 1797.

Saw mill.   Floor.

Fly Wheel

Saw Frame

W E L L

CISTERN

Pump

46. *Above right* Among the very few pieces of mechanical equipment available before 1797 were treadwheel cranes. This is the last naval one (photographed in 1965, before restoration), formerly in use in Harwich dockyard. Design of these changed little during the seventeenth and eighteenth centuries.

47. *Right* Portsmouth Dockyard. The first dock pump to be powered by a steam engine was this one installed in 1797. (see plate 12)

48. The elaborate carving and gilding on the stern of HMS *Victory*. Such decoration lasted well into the nineteenth century and was only stifled by the introduction of metal warships. Each dockyard until then had its small complement of carvers and gilders.

set of basins anywhere (43). Later, it was the turn of Malta and then at the end of the nineteenth century Gibraltar had its first set of dry-docks. The last major group were constructed at Singapore in the 1930s; ironically the largest dry-dock there was completed just in time to receive HMS *Prince of Wales* a few days before she was sunk by the Japanese.

Chapter 3

Manufacturing within the Dockyards

Within the home dockyards, generally a little removed from activities centred on the building slips and dry-docks, were further extensive areas used for manufacturing as distinct from storage purposes. For although to a casual observer warship construction was the most obvious and dramatic function of a royal dockyard, this was only one facet of its operations. Once the bare wooden hull of a warship had been launched from a slip or floated out of a dry-dock, it needed its masts to be stepped and a host of fittings and equipment to be installed, while subsequent maintenance and repairs could easily eclipse its prime construction cost. Royal dockyards too, although usually building only the larger ships of the line, generally were responsible for most of the fittings and items of equipment for warships under construction in merchants' yards, while the subsequent maintenance of these latter vessels was naturally the responsibility of the government establishments.

Before the growth of large-scale industry and efficient inland transport in the form of a railway network, it was inevitable that dockyards should manufacture most of the items required by a warship, although outside suppliers, especially during wartime peaks of activity, always played a significant part. The bulk of supplies bought by the Navy Board, for most of its life probably the major purchasing department of government,

49. *Right* Portsmouth Dockyard. The boat pond and 5, 6 and 7 boathouses. In its present form the boat pond is eighteenth-century. The two timber boathouses, although nineteenth-century, are typical of such structures which were common in all the dockyards from early on. The brick 6 boathouse dates from c. 1844.

50. *Opposite top* Portsmouth Dockyard. Inside 7 boathouse in 1981. Such buildings were used for repairing and storing as well as building ships' boats.

51. *Opposite bottom* Portsmouth Dockyard. Inside 6 boathouse showing the massive internal construction considered necessary to carry boats stored on the floor above.

52. *Top right* Chatham Dockyard. The end of the Lower Boat Store, a mid-nineteenth century timber-framed building. Although humble, this had architectural aspirations, most notably in its well-proportioned windows.

53. *Right* Portsmouth Dockyard. One of a set of four handsome workshops and stores erected between 1786 and 1790 in the centre of the yard.

arrived at the dockyards as raw material or in a part-finished state. Timber and hemp were prime examples of the former, while pig and wrought iron and bales of canvas were typical of the latter. Excluding the preparation and assembly of timber used for a warship's hull, substantial manufacturing activities centred on four main materials: wood, metal, canvas and hemp. More than a century of all-metal warships has inevitably meant the decline of older craft skills, the disappearance of some and the rise of new ones, but if skills have changed, many buildings belonging to this earlier age remain, often adapted to uses undreamed of by their original inhabitants.

A very few buildings continued their original functions well into the

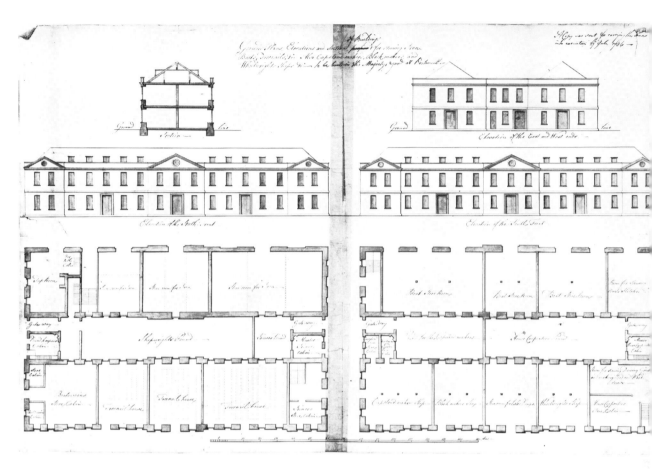

54. Portsmouth Dockyard. The original design for a storehouse and workshops matching the building in plate 53. This one had iron, treenails and ships' pumps kept in it and provided working space for capstan makers, block makers and wheelwrights. The craft of the wheelwright was still alive in Chatham Dockyard in 1983.

twentieth century. The blockmills at Portsmouth retained a manufacturing capacity into the 1960s and at Chatham it was possible to see the early nineteenth-century smithery still operating into the 1970s and to savour something of the atmosphere which moved Charles Dickens to describe it in *The Uncommercial Traveller* (**58**). Nearby, the Colour Loft continues a tradition of flag making which in all probability goes back to the completion of this building as a sail loft in the mid 1720s (**60**).

Perhaps most fascinating of all is the great eighteenth-century ropery at Chatham. The recent cessation of Ministry of Defence manufacturing here ended a tradition of naval ropemaking unbroken since the reign of James I. At the time of writing a private firm has taken over and it is to be hoped that the skills and craftsmanship of the ropemakers and their carefully maintained Victorian and Georgian machines, some of the latter over 170 years old, will continue in production in this extraordinary 1140-feet-long building (**68**).

Of all dockyard skills, that of timber working suffered the fastest eclipse relative to other trades when metal warships were introduced in the 1860s. Shipwrights were most immediately affected, but repercussions were felt all over the dockyards away from the shipbuilding slips. Wood was used

55. *Below* A scene inside the now vanished Devonport masthouse at the end of the nineteenth century. The Chatham masthouse and mould loft has a very similar interior (**29, 30**).

56. *Opposite top* By the end of the eighteenth century a shortage of suitable timber led to experiments with wrought iron straps for strengthening hulls and the substitution of iron knees for oak ones. The frigate *Unicorn* shown here, now being restored at Dundee, was built at Chatham in the 1820s and used iron extensively. Such developments brought much extra work to dockyard smitheries.

for decks, masts, spars, ships' boats, panelling and most internal fittings as well as most spectacularly in the great carved figureheads and elaborate decoration around the stern quarters. Probably the most highly skilled woodworkers outside the immediate ranks of shipwrights were the mastmakers and carvers, while the joiners and house carpenters had additional responsibilities for maintaining and sometimes constructing dockyard buildings.

With the exception of the mastmakers, none of these craftsmen needed specially designed workshops. Often they worked in single-storey timber-framed buildings clad in weatherboarding with slate or tile roofs. The two late nineteenth-century boathouses flanking the boat pond at Portsmouth and the Lower Boat Store at Chatham are typical if now rare examples of this ubiquitous type of dockyard structure (**49–52**). Few craftsmen were as well housed as the Portsmouth house carpenters, joiners and carvers who moved into handsome new two-storey brick-built workshops in the centre of the dockyard in the 1780s. These buildings still survive although alterations and infilling of the open space between them—an open space once used to season timber—has destroyed the formal architectural composition of this area.

57. *Below* Among the heaviest jobs tackled by naval smitheries were construction of the huge iron anchors. The larger yards had smitheries entirely devoted to this work. By 1816, the date of this print, mechanical aids were still limited to hand bellows, small cranes and primitive drop-hammers although steam blowing-engines had been suggested several years earlier.

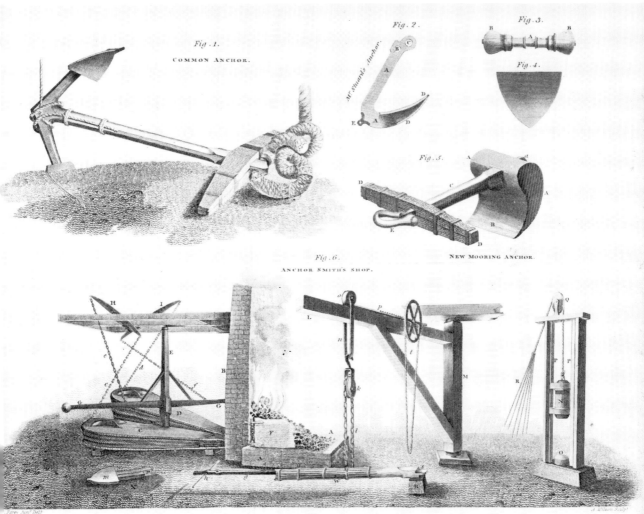

Fig. 1.
COMMON ANCHOR.

Fig. 2.
Mc Stuart's Anchor.

Fig. 3.

Fig. 4.

Fig. 5.

NEW MOORING ANCHOR.

Fig. 6.
ANCHOR SMITH'S SHOP.

65

58. Chatham Smithery. Edward Holl's 1806 design. Much of this building remains, continuing in use into the early 1970s. It now contains a rare collection of smiths' equipment dating back to the nineteenth century.

Some 40 years earlier the Chatham carpenters and joiners, fewer in number, had had a new three-storey workshop built for them. Its careful design and detailing, sadly marred by more recent generations, is accounted for by proximity to the officers' terrace. When this workshop proved inadequate to house powered machinery in the mid-nineteenth century, a larger two-storey workshop was built adjacent to it, remaining in use until the closure of the dockyard.

Chatham too has the last surviving example of a timber masthouse, erected by yard shipwrights and carpenters between 1753 and 1755. With the main mast of a first-rate exceeding 100 feet in length, such buildings needed to be long and to be adjacent to the mast ponds where the fir trunks were stored under water until required to prevent drying-out and splitting. The Chatham building could accommodate masts up to 120 feet long and, as mentioned in Chapter 2, incorporates a mould loft above its centre bays (29).

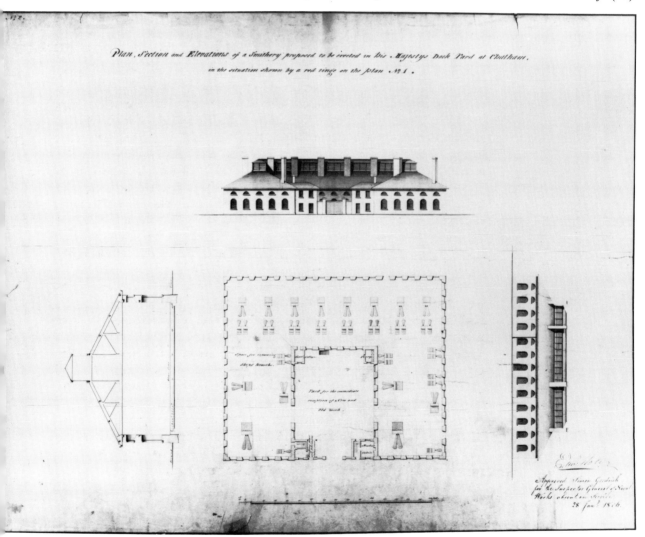

59. At the smaller overseas bases there was no need for the large and elaborate smitheries essential to the major home dockyards. This former smiths' shop at Antigua is indistinguishable from an ordinary village smithy.

Apart from sawpits, mastmakers required no other fixtures, new masts being shaped and jointed on a series of trestles.

From the earliest, dockyards employed smiths to prepare the numerous pieces of ironwork needed on ships. Smitheries—a peculiarly dockyard term—were frequently divided into two distinct types. By the beginning of the nineteenth century the largest metal items on a warship, apart from the guns, were the wrought iron anchors and the major dockyards had smitheries entirely devoted to their manufacture and repair. Anchor smiths tended to be a breed apart, but their buildings and equipment were similar to normal smitheries. The latter produced the multifarious metal objects from mast hoops to hinges. In the early nineteenth century under the influence of Sir Robert Seppings' work at Chatham, iron knees (56) began to supersede the increasingly scarce oak ones and heavy wrought iron diagonal braces were used to stiffen hulls. All of this meant further and welcome work for the smitheries, which were also in some dockyards handling the copper sheets introduced on a general scale for hull sheathing in the 1780s.

There were few, if any, wrought or forged items the larger smitheries were unable to tackle, from links of anchor chain to parts for ships' pumps, but not until the mid-nineteenth century did they have smelting furnaces necessary for founding. Metal warships driven by machinery revolutionised metal working in the dockyards, leading to construction of vast foundries at Portsmouth and Devonport with specialist steam-powered equipment capable of everything from shaping hull plates to casting intricate parts for engines. Patternmakers and mouldmakers became essential members of the foundry teams with their own work areas close to the casting floors. Lesser dockyards and overseas bases, with the exception of Malta and Gibraltar at the end of the nineteenth century, were not expected to tackle such heavy work and their facilities remained correspondingly less sophisticated.

Probably the earliest smithery to survive, albeit in an incomplete condition, is the tiny one no larger than a village blacksmith's shop at Antigua

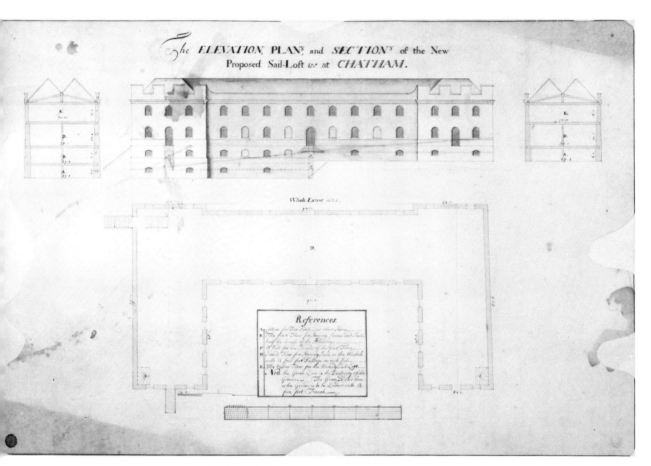

The ELEVATION, PLANS and SECTIONS of the New
Proposed Sail-Loft &c at CHATHAM.

Whole Extent

References.

60. Chatham Dockyard. A plan of the proposed brick sail loft built here in the 1720s. This is the oldest surviving sail loft in a royal dockyard. Only on the top floor could the central structural supports be omitted to give a clear floor space for the sailmakers. The lower floors were used to store canvas and completed sails. Colours are still made here.

dockyard, but this is scarcely typical (**59**). The square two-storey North Office Block at Portsmouth is a conversion of a smithery built at the then northern boundary of the dockyard in 1791, but the most interesting one to remain is No 1 Smithery at Chatham. This was begun in 1806 to a design by Edward Holl and originally consisted of three ranges round an open court-yard approached from the west past two lodges. In the mid-nineteenth century and on several subsequent occasions this was adapted and expanded, remaining in use until the 1970s. At the time of writing it still contains much early and now rare equipment ranging from a locksmith's workshop to huge steam hammers (**58**). South Yard Devonport has a rather later smithery more typical of mid-nineteenth century design with its metal-framed roof and generous provision of windows.

Excluding the effects of enemy action, the most vulnerable areas of a warship were her sails and rigging. With care and luck, suits of sails could last for years, but both they and the standing and running rigging were comparatively fragile and generally subject to more rapid deterioration than the rest of the vessel. Not surprisingly, every home dockyard had its complement of sailmakers, while the larger yards had purpose-designed buildings devoted to their exclusive use where bales of canvas were stock-

68

piled and where new sails could be cut and stitched and stored to await issue. Sailmaking required only hand tools and large unencumbered floor areas where lengths of canvas could be laid out and stitched to form the great mainsails. Such floor space was most easily provided on the top floors of buildings where structural supports could be kept to a minimum, giving rise to the term *sail loft*. Often most of the building was used for quite a different purpose, this purpose appearing in the records, sometimes making sail lofts difficult to trace. Until its destruction in the earthquake of 1843, the sail loft at Antigua dockyard was above the boathouse. At Portsmouth a new sail loft was authorised 'upon the taphouse shed' in 1744. In spite of its title of shed, this was no mean building, measuring some 96 feet by 37 feet, and proving adequate until the 1780s when the sailmakers were ordered to move to premises on a floor in the new rigging house then building on what is now South Camber.

The only purpose-built sail loft to survive intact in a home dockyard is at Chatham where it was built in the early 1720s as a combined canvas store and sail workshop. It is a long three-storey brick building with twin lofts and the sailmakers' room on the floor below. The wooden pillars sup-

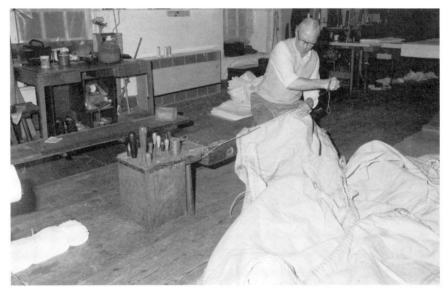

61. *Above right* At work in Chatham sail loft in 1981. Note the sailmaker's bench.

62. *Right* Bales of sisal inside the 1728 hemp house at Chatham in December 1981. Note the board lined walls and almost total absence of windows to help maintain a dry, even temperature.

63. *Above* At work in the Chatham spinning room c. 1900. Machinery was then steam-powered from overhead line shafts; the latter are still in place. For long, women's jobs in naval roperies were reserved for widows of seamen.

porting the first floor are re-used ribs from a seventeenth-century warship which must have been being broken-up in the dockyard at the time. More recently the building has been used exclusively as a colour loft producing the full range of flags needed by the navy for ordinary use and for special occasions (**60, 61**).

Probably the last sail loft ever built for the navy is at Bermuda dockyard. Constructed at the very time—1860—that the huge foundry/machine shop complex for the new steam navy was taking shape at Devonport, the Bermuda sail loft is a two-storey stone building with the luxury, possibly unique in naval sail lofts, of a splinter-proof teak floor. At overseas bases in quieter parts of the world, sailing warships continued to serve long after they had been relegated from the main battle fleets so the Bermuda sail loft undoubtedly proved useful, although in the later stages of the dockyard's life it was chiefly famed for being the best dance floor on the islands.

There is no difficulty in identifying naval roperies for their enormous spinning and laying houses are the longest and most distinctive of naval buildings. Until well into the nineteenth century all but the largest commercial ropemakers with substantial capital invariably used open-air ropewalks for spinning and laying, in spite of dislocations caused by bad weather. But naval dockyards, with their greater capital resources and a need for reliable production, began to establish rope houses in the seventeenth century. Woolwich was first in 1612, Chatham followed in 1618 then Portsmouth and finally Plymouth Dock where a ropery formed part of the original plan of 1690. By then, the principal buildings were already up to 1,000 feet long so reasons of space as well as finance dictated that cordage production was concentrated at these four home dockyards alone. Short-lived roperies were to be established at Port Mahon, where there was an open-air ropewalk for part of the eighteenth century, and at Malta in the early nineteenth, but these were on nothing like the scale of the main ones.

Cordage manufacture involved several distinct processes each requiring their own buildings which for convenience were naturally grouped

64. *Opposite below* Portsmouth Dockyard. The late-eighteenth-century covered way connecting the hemp house and hatchelling house on the right with the 1770 double ropehouse on the left. Hemp was hatchelled – its fibres were straightened and untangled – before being taken to the spinners on the upper floors of the double ropehouses at Portsmouth and Chatham.

65. *Above right* Portsmouth double ropehouse photographed in 1942 before modernisation. Ropemaking ceased here in the 1860s. This ropehouse was the model for the 1786 one at Chatham and was one of the first to have upper floors for spinners, hence the term 'double ropehouse'. Hitherto, spinners sometimes had their own separate building parallel to the ropery.

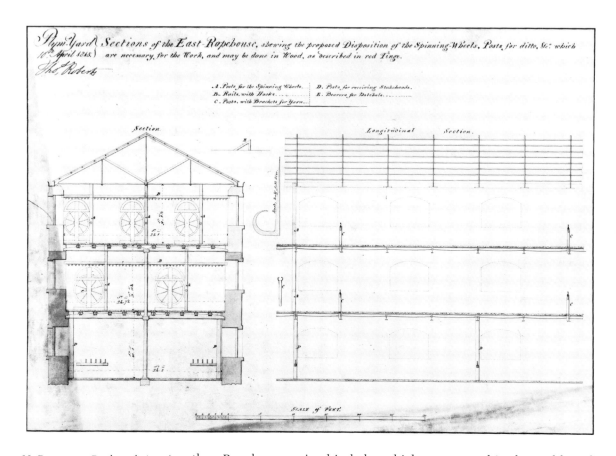

Plym. Yard } Sections of the East Ropehouse, shewing the proposed Disposition of the Spinning Wheels, Posts for ditto, &c: which
16th April 1815 } are necessary for the Work, and may be done in Wood, as described in red Tinge.

Tho. Roberts

A. Posts for the Spinning Wheels.   D. Posts for receiving Stakeheads.
B. Rails with Hooks.   E. Bearers for Ratchels.
C. Posts with Brackets for Yarn.

Section   Longitudinal   Section.

SCALE of FEET.

66. Devonport Dockyard. A cross-section of the spinning house, renamed the east ropehouse, in 1815. Clearly visible are the spinning frames on the upper floors. This building, constructed in 1763, was gutted by fire in 1812. It was rebuilt as a fireproof structure by Edward Holl who replaced timber structural members with cast and wrought iron and used York stone for the upper floors. Part of this building survived the blitz.

together. Raw hemp arrived in bales which were stored in the cool board-lined interiors of hemp houses (62). From there hemp was taken to have its fibres straightened, untangled and graded by length by being hatchelled—drawn across rows of spikes on boards—in a hatchelling house. This latter was almost invariably sited at one end of the spinning room. Spinners then attached sorted bundles of fibres weighing up to 65 pounds round their waists, attached ends of fibres to a revolving hook on a manually-turned spinning frame and produced yarns by walking backwards down the length of the spinning floor. An experienced spinner could produce a thousand-foot yarn in approximately twelve minutes. Bundles or hauls containing 400 yarns were then carried to a white yarn house to await their turn for impregnating with tar. This was done by passing the hauls at a regular speed through a tar kettle kept at an exact temperature—too hot and the fibres absorbed too much and were weakened, too little and only the outer ones were coated. Now black, the yarns were hung to dry in a black yarn house before the final stages of ropemaking. Tarring was the first part of the ropemaking process to use other than human muscle, for by the late-eighteenth century horse gins powered the capstans feeding yarns through the tar kettles. Evidence for these remains at Chatham and Devonport (70).

The final and most dramatic stages of manufacture took place on the

67. Devonport Dockyard. The ropeyard as rebuilt between 1763 and 1771. Prominent are the spinning and laying houses, each 1200 feet long. On the right are the yarn stores and tarring house. The laying house on the left was totally destroyed in the 1939–45 war; the hemp houses beyond it were badly damaged. From the 1774 model in the National Maritime Museum.

laying floor. Here the yarns, by now on reels arranged in banks at one end, were attached to further sets of revolving hooks on laying or forming machines which travelled the length of the laying floor twisting the yarns together as strands. In 1799 Captain Joseph Huddart patented equipment which markedly improved this part of the process: before being attached to the hooks on the forming machines the yarns were fed through holes in a perforated metal plate and then through a tubular die. This ensured that every yarn was in equal tension, and the strands formed a true circular cross section, making for much stronger and more uniform cordage. This invention was promptly adopted in all naval roperies and the original equipment remains at Chatham.

Strands, which might contain twenty yarns, were then attached to hooks on a further pair of machines, one fixed at one end of the laying floor, the second on wheels at the other. Between the two was a top-cart, a movable carriage carrying sets of horizontal wooden cones with grooves running their lengths. If it was a three-inch hawser-laid rope being manufactured, each of the three strands forming it was attached to individual hooks on the fixed machine, then led over the grooves on a top, by now at the far end of the laying floor adjacent to the movable laying machine. The three strands were attached to a single hook on the latter; when this

68. *Right* The southern end of Chatham Dockyard in 1982. Behind the great warehouses on Anchor Wharf is the 1140 feet of the double ropehouse begun in 1786. To its right are the hemp and yarn stores.

69. *Below* Looking along the immense laying floor at Chatham. Here the yarns prepared on the spinning floor are laid into ropes and cables using machinery installed here in 1811 and 1854. A photograph taken in 1983 shortly before the end of Ministry of Defence production.

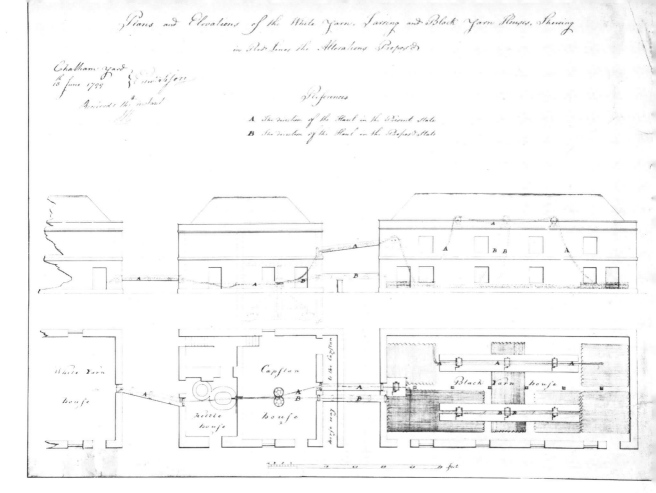

Plans and Elevations of the White Yarn, Tarring and Black Yarn Houses, Shewing in Red Lines the Alterations Proposd

70. *Above* The Chatham yarn houses. A 1799 drawing showing the method of operation. White yarns received from the spinners were stored in the building on the left before being pulled through a tar kettle by a horse powered capstan. They were then hung to dry in the black yarn house before being placed on spools and being taken to the ropery laying floor. All these Chatham buildings still exist.

71. *Right* Devonport Dockyard. Capstans in the roof space of one of the black yarn houses. These helped distribute the hauls of black yarn evenly throughout the building.

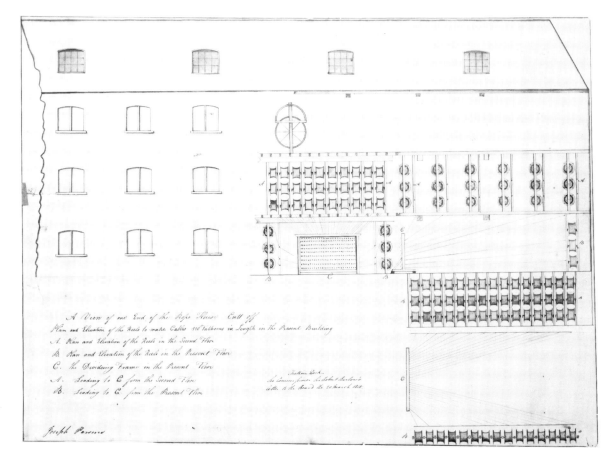

A View of one End of the Rope House Cut off

Plan and Elevation of the Reels to make Cables 116 fathoms in Length in the Present Building

A. Plan and Elevation of the Reels in the Second Floor

B. Plan and Elevation of the Reels in the Present Floor

C. The Dividing Frames in the Present Floor

A. Leading to C from the Second Floor

B. Leading to C from the Present Floor

Chatham Dock
The Commissioners Robert Barlow
to be laid the 20 March 1818

Joseph Parsons

72. *Above* One end of the Chatham ropehouse in the early nineteenth century, showing yarns being fed from spools through to the forming machines.

73. *Right* One of a set of forming machines built by Henry Maudslay's London factory and delivered to Chatham ropery in 1811. They have remained in daily use for 172 years.

revolved, twisting the three strands into one rope, the latter gradually forced the top-cart down the laying floor, the laying machine following it at a slower pace as the twisting process gradually taughtened and shortened the rope. To maintain tension and prevent the completed product unravelling, the direction of twist was reversed at each stage of the process.

Cordage was sized by circumference, naval roperies producing everything from the finest sail twine to 24-inch anchor cables. By the end of the eighteenth century three different sized sets of forming and laying machines were in use. These were hauled the length of the laying floor by huge man-powered winches fixed at both ends of the building; up to 220 men—some brought in from elsewhere in the dockyard—would be employed in the final stages of laying a 24-inch cable, 59 men manning the winches. The Navy Board's very real fear of fire in a ropery meant that steam engines were not used before 1836 when one was installed at Chatham, enabling some reduction in laying-floor manpower and reducing strain on the ropemakers.

To produce the longest unspliced cables required by the fleet meant that from the first spinning and laying houses had to be of immense length. 900 feet was unexceptional by the late seventeenth century. In the mid-eighteenth century Plymouth built twin spinning and laying houses 1200 feet long; Portsmouth, plagued by dockyard fires in 1760, 1770 and 1776, and short of land, built a combined spinning and laying house in 1770, spinners on the upper floors, known as a double ropehouse. This was 1030 feet long and was the model for Chatham when the latter replaced its wooden spinning and laying houses in the late 1780s.

Woolwich and Portsmouth roperies ceased production in the 1860s, but nearly all the buildings of the latter survive as storehouses. Devonport remained in production until blitzed in 1941. There, only part of the spinning house, rebuilt after a fire in 1812, remains along with the tarring and yarn houses and the master ropemaker's house of 1772. Only Chatham is still complete. Here, although the earliest hemp house dates from 1728, the bulk of the buildings were reconstructed between 1786 and 1792 and an engine house, which still contains the frame of the beam engine, was added in 1836. With the exception of modern spinning machinery installed on a first floor added to the hemp houses, all the main ropemaking machinery here dates from 1811 and 1854. When Ministry of Defence production ceased here at the end of February 1983 it marked the end of government manufacturing of cordage for the Royal Navy which in Chatham's case had been unbroken since 1618 (**69, 73**).

A modern warship has comparatively modest cordage requirements so that it is not always immediately apparent just how important the dockyard roperies were in their heyday. But at the time of Trafalgar a third-rate of 74 guns, the most numerous class of line-of-battleship, needed cordage varying in circumference from $\frac{3}{4}$ inch to $18\frac{1}{2}$ inches. The lengths varied from 78 feet of 10-inch to nearly 27,000 feet of 3-inch; seven circumferences were needed in totals of more than 10,000 feet apiece and these are figures

74. *Above* Portsmouth Dockyard. The Block Mills built between 1802 and 1806 originally to house some of Bentham's woodworking machinery which was to be powered by the steam engine in plate 12. By 1808 Marc Isambard Brunel's machinery to manufacture ships' blocks had been installed in the specially built range in the centre. This has been described as the world's first use of machine tools for mass production.

75. *Right* A partly formed shell for a double block on one of Brunel's cornering saws. A 1965 photograph.

76. *Far right* Brunel's saw for the *lignum vitae* sheeves for the blocks.

which relate to standing and running rigging only. Like sails, cordage had a limited life and needed renewal every few years. To the sailing navy, roperies, mast houses and sail lofts were what machine and boiler shops were to be to the steam-driven navy of the late nineteenth century.

Outside the four principal dockyard skills centred on shipwrights, smiths, sail-and ropemakers were other more specialist crafts and workshops, many of which have left no trace at all. The craft of oarmaker, for example, could be carried on in the corner of virtually any building and would leave no evidence for its existence once the craftsmen departed. Similarly, painters' shops were no more than ordinary storehouses, or might even be just wooden sheds. But in one or two cases there remain workshops whose products or methods of operation were so specialised that a single building in one dockyard could supply the fleet. Such workshops date from the early years of the dockyard's own industrial revolution which effectively began in 1795 with the appointment of Brigadier-General Sir Samuel Bentham. Little might have been heard of him or his work had he not had the good fortune to meet and recognise the talents of Marc

77. Brunel's sawmill at Chatham begun in 1811 and completed in 1814.

horizontal section of the Painters Shop and lead Mill.

Isambard Brunel and to use the skills of Henry Maudslay's south London factory to construct much of the new machinery.

Bentham's own particular interest and expertise was in powered wood-working machinery. With Admiralty backing, he had constructed twin parallel ranges of three-storey brick workshops on vaults over the former North Basin at Portsmouth Dockyard. This basin, constructed in the 1690s, had long been used as a sump or reservoir to drain adjacent dry-docks. Bentham replaced the existing horse-gin pumps here with a steam engine which by day powered his woodworking machinery and by night emptied the reservoir. Few details are known of his machinery, but in 1802 the project was transformed.

Obtaining Admiralty approval to purchase equipment designed by Marc Brunel to mass-produce ships' blocks, Bentham linked the two ranges with a single-storey factory to contain the new machinery which was manufactured to Brunel's specifications by Henry Maudslay. Between 1802 and 1806 three groups totalling 45 machines were installed here capable of manufacturing all sizes of blocks. By 1808, 130,000 blocks were being turned out annually in what is claimed to be the first factory in the world to use machine tools for mass-production. Ten machinists replaced the jobs of 110 skilled blockmakers and the Admiralty was able to end its contracts with outside suppliers (**74, 75, 76**).

The blockmills are justifiably famous in their own right, with sets of their machinery in the Science Museum, London and the Smithsonian in Washington, but part of their importance lay in encouraging the Navy Board to experiment further with mechanisation. The set of four forming machines built by Henry Maudslay in 1811 for Chatham ropery was part of this process (**73**) as was the 1812 Brunel sawmill in the same yard (**77**). But in Georgian dockyards the number of simple repetitive tasks suitable for mechanising were small given the power of contemporary steam engines and limits to machine tool technology. With sawing, pumping and block-making the most obvious tasks had been modernised. However, in 1817 the Navy Board authorised a lead and paint mill at Chatham. Although conservative in appearance, Holl's design is wholly fireproof. Behind its brick exterior he used a combination of cast iron pillars, iron beams and York stone paving for the upper floors, wrought and cast iron roof trusses, iron window frames and cast iron doors. A small wing on the west side housed a beam engine which powered a lead rolling mill and a series of grinders and mixers for paint-making. The first floor above the paint manufacturing end was equipped with a series of adjustable iron frames on which canvas could be stretched for painting. These still remain as do traces of the overhead line shafting and marks of the beam engine (**78**).

Completion of the Chatham lead mill marks the end of Georgian factory innovations in the dockyards, although the Victualling Board made extensive use of steam-powered machinery during modernisation of its own facilities at Gosport and Plymouth in the 1820s and 1830s. It was to be Portsmouth, though, which first felt the effects of the new generation

78. *Opposite top* The Chatham lead and paint mill. Designed as a fireproof building by Edward Holl in 1818 for producing paint and sheet lead. The adjustable iron frames on the upper floor were for stretching canvas prior to painting. Both building and canvas frames remain and can be seen on the near right in plate 68.

79. *Opposite bottom* Portsmouth 2 Ship Shop, completed in 1848 as a manufacturing and repair shop for machinery for steam vessels. Its vast scale dwarfs nearby Georgian buildings. In front is the contemporary basin.

of steam-assisted warships which made their appearance on a significant scale in the 1840s. In 1843 work started on construction of the Great Steam Basin, now 2 Basin, at the then north end of the dockyard. Along the western side was built a factory equipped to service the machinery on board these new vessels. Now known as 2 Ship Shop, its handsome elevations dominate this part of the dockyard, while within, use of iron as a structural material removed the need for columns and allowed maximum flexibility of use (**79**). A large iron and brass foundry followed a few years later on the southern side of the basin (**24**). The scale of these two buildings sets them apart from all earlier dockyard factories; only the great roperies could compete in size.

In 1844 work began at Devonport on an even more ambitious expansion, creating a complete new dockyard, known as North Yard to distinguish it from the Georgian dockyard, renamed South Yard. The massive civil engineering works needed to excavate the basin and dry-docks were under the supervision of William Scamp and Colonel Green. Next to the basin was built a huge factory—in reality a complex of machine shops, stores, pattern shops and offices grouped round a very large foundry. This was centralisation of manufacturing and storage facilities carried to new lengths. Covering several acres, the granite and limestone elevations of this great rectangular complex, with their bold decoration and detailing, are the nearest the royal dockyards have ever come to expressing a pride in Empire. Behind the confident façades, though, great care was taken to use the most modern construction methods to give flexibility of use, while away from the public gaze, stock bricks replaced expensive stone.

The cost of the Devonport factory led to questions in Parliament and was not repeated when Chatham dockyard reclaimed St Mary's Creek and laid out an even larger set of three wet-docks with attendant dry-docks. Factory buildings for the Medway yard, grouped at the head of the dry-docks, were formed from iron slip housings originally erected at Woolwich dockyard (**43**). Only later, at Malta and Gibraltar, where building stone was cheap, did the navy repeat on a reduced scale the elaboration of the Devonport factory (**21**).

Chapter 4
Naval Warehouses

When Daniel Defoe visited Chatham dockyard in the early 1720s he was deeply struck by the 'streets of warehouses and storehouses for laying up the naval treasure', describing them with some exaggeration as 'the largest in dimension, and the most in number that are anywhere to be seen in the world'. Today, successors of these buildings do much to preserve the Georgian atmosphere in the hearts of Chatham and Portsmouth, for no other class of building was required in such large numbers by the Royal Navy (**4**, **9**, **68**, **83**). The theory was sound: well-filled stores were there to enable the fleet to operate swiftly and efficiently when needed.

Of course, in practice few governments, least of all seventeenth- and eighteenth-century ones, provided sufficient funds in peacetime to maintain such reserves, but it is a testimony to the farsightedness of Navy Board officials in the last 40 years of the eighteenth century that the storehouses planned and built then remained adequate throughout the nineteenth century and continue in many cases to supply the fleet today.

By 1700, the older dockyards were cramped and many of their facilities

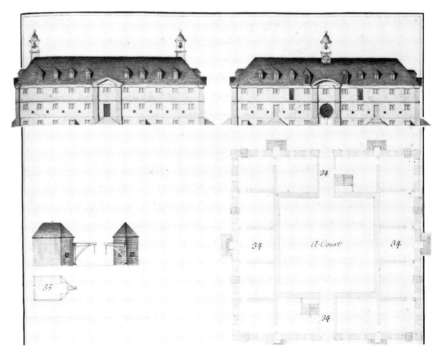

80. Plymouth Dockyard. The Great Storehouse of 1692, a quadrangular building containing numerous small rooms, many difficult of access. Its west range survived into the nineteenth century. Its design was typical of the larger naval storehouses of the late seventeenth century.

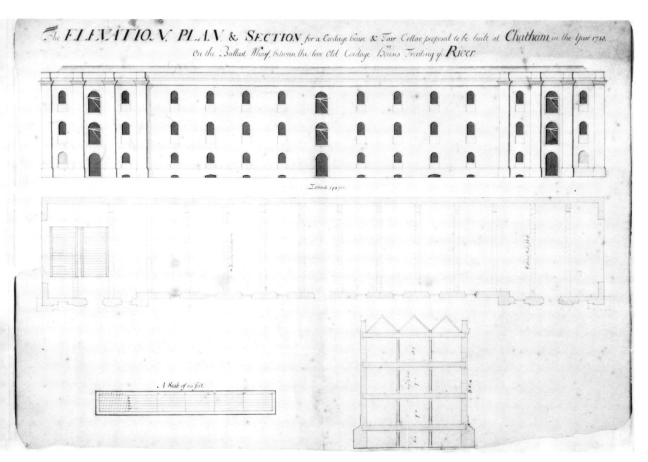

The ELEVATION PLAN & SECTION *for a Cordage house & Tarr Cellar, proposed to be built at* Chatham, *in the Year 1718.*
On the Ballast Wharf, between the two Old Cordage houses Fronting y River.

A Scale of 100 feet.

81. The cordage house and tar cellars built at Chatham in 1718. With generous access to all floors and minimal internal obstructions it was the prototype of modern naval storehouses. It was demolished in the 1780s.

were outmoded. Perhaps nowhere was this more apparent than in the design of their storehouses. These were generally small with access to cramped rooms frequently up steps and through narrow doorways. Goods for upper floors usually had to be manhandled up and down flights of stairs. Such design bred inefficiency; new stock tended to be piled on older material and used first, receipt and issue were casual and pilfering was all too easy, while the rigid layout of such buildings made rearrangement for different types of stores virtually impossible. Not surprisingly, official correspondence is full of reports of decayed materials, missing stock and inadequate records.

At Plymouth Dock in the 1690s an attempt was made to remedy some of these design deficiencies. Here, one great quadrangular storehouse, the Great Storehouse, served the needs of the fledgling dockyard. It also contained space for the rigging from 30 warships of third-rate or less, a reflection of the original intention to use Plymouth as a cruiser base. But in spite of wall cranes and rollers for easier stowing of cordage, this building still had many of the drawbacks of its predecessors. Short flights of steps still led to narrow ground-floor doorways, while within, load-bearing walls divided the interior into a series of comparatively small spaces (**80**).

Not until 1717 did the Navy Board sanction construction of a design containing the essential elements of all good dockyard warehouses: ease of goods access and flexibility of use. This was a new cordage house on what is now Anchor Wharf, Chatham. 194 feet long and 35 feet wide, it had three storeys and vaulted fireproof cellars. Three sets of wide doorways served each floor, each set of doorways with their own wall cranes. Inside there were no fixed partitions, allowing maximum freedom to the storekeeper (31).

The best features of the Chatham cordage house were to be widely adopted in most subsequent naval storehouses. In the course of the next hundred years such buildings grew considerably in size while conscious efforts were made to site them according to their functions. A typical late eighteenth-century naval storehouse had three storeys, often over barrel-vaulted cellars, and was built of brick or stone with a tiled or slated roof.

Interiors usually had board-lined walls with twin rows of sturdy wooden pillars supporting upper floors. Larger buildings had cross-walls, partly for strength, partly in the hope of containing the spread of fire. If external wall cranes were not provided, the main staircase was invariably built round a capacious central well containing a block and tackle for hoisting heavy or bulky goods to the upper floors. However, no eighteenth-century dockyard storehouse seems to have been as well-equipped as the two completed for the Board of Ordnance at Morice Yard, Plymouth Dock, in 1724. These, which still remain, boasted wooden railways on their ground floors in addition to wall cranes (142).

Very few naval goods and materials needed really specialised storage, although hemp houses tended to have the minimum of windows, all carefully shuttered to maintain an even temperature within. Flammable materials such as whale oil, paint and tar posed the biggest hazards. Where possible, these were stored in vaulted cellars with access independent of the building above. Such cellars are features of the roperies at Chatham and Devonport and were incorporated under 9, 10 and 11 Stores at Portsmouth (83, 84).

Nearly all the surviving eighteenth-century storehouses were planned and mostly built in the 25 years after 1760 which meant that the bulk were completed before the development of fireproof construction using cast and wrought iron to replace timber structural members and stone flags to replace wooden floorboards. Had such a system been available and been proven, there seems little doubt that the Navy Board would have used it, despite higher cost, for their fear of fire was endemic. Instead, when finance permitted, they replaced timber buildings with ones of brick or stone, not only a better long-term investment, but also as a means of lessening the potential spread of fire. In the 1780s they flirted briefly with a scheme for thin metal plates nailed to the undersides of joists and floorboards as an alleged fireproofing, but the practice was neither satisfactory nor widespread, although some survive in 9, 10 and 11 Stores at Portsmouth.

Apart from vaulted cellars, the only totally fireproof building earlier

82. The Chatham clock-tower building on the 1774 dockyard model at the National Maritime Museum. The sawpits were infilled in 1803 when the upper floors were rebuilt in brick.

83. Portsmouth Dockyard. 9, 10 and 11 Stores, built between 1764 and 1784 and arguably the most handsome of all naval store-houses, despite the loss of the clocktower from the roof of 10 Store.

than 1800 is the former pay-office in Portsmouth. Here, the need to keep records and large sums of money secure led to a curious hybrid design where crudely-detailed cast iron columns support quadripartite brick vaulting. Although in a sense a storehouse, this was small and atypical of such buildings. Its exact date of construction is unknown, but it may date from the late 1790s (89).

The great dockyard rebuilding and expansion schemes under way from the 1760s attempted to rationalise dockyard planning, somewhat neglected since Dummer's work at Plymouth Dock in the 1690s, and to group store-houses according to use. Storehouses used invariably for a single type of material were in practice limited to the roperies where it was logical to group hemp and yarn stores adjacent to the spinning and laying rooms. In the remainder of the yards storehouses had three broad functions: general stores, lay-apart stores and present-use stores.

As the title implies, general stores contained the multiplicity of raw materials and finished products needed by dockyards and were generally sited near to manufacturing areas. Each store could have a wide variety of contents and well into the eighteenth century might be combined with a workshop under the same roof. Such is how the Clocktower building at Chatham started life in 1723. This is the oldest surviving dockyard storehouse, but originally combined that function with sawpits at one end of the ground floor (**31, 82**). A much later and very much larger example, also at Chatham, is the combined storehouse and fitted rigging house on Anchor Wharf. Completed in the year of Trafalgar and over 600 feet long, half was devoted to general storage, including completed cordage from the adjacent ropery, and half was used by the riggers preparing sets of cordage in advance for each class of warship (**68**).

84. Portsmouth Dockyard. 10 Store, the 1776 drawing.

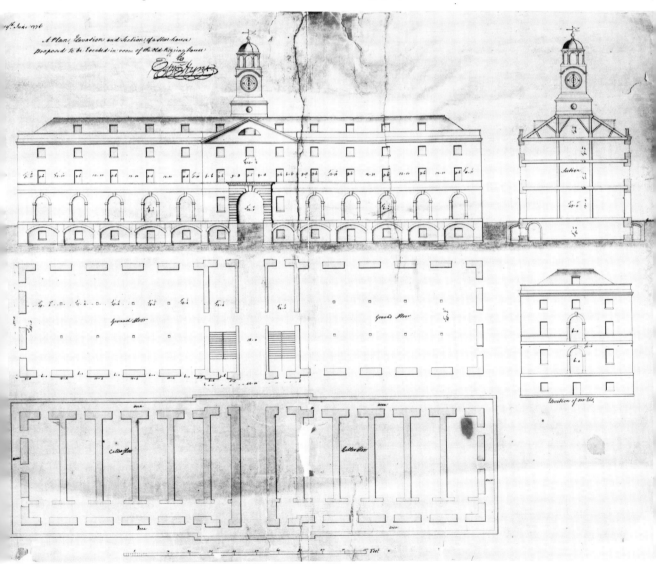

85. *Above* A detail of one of the plain and functional staircases inside one of the late-eighteenth-century Georgian storehouses at Portsmouth, in this case 19 Store.

86. *Above right* Portsmouth Dockyard. Inside 10 Store, showing the simple and sturdy construction.

Lay-apart stores were divided internally by wooden partitions, each space or series of compartments used for equipment from a particular warship in ordinary or undergoing refit. Sails, standing and running rigging and spare cables, all better preserved ashore, formed the bulk of items in this category. Such storehouses are probably as old as the permanent navy, one such in 1547 becoming the first building to be hired for warships wintering in the Medway, its acquisition traditionally marking the beginning of Chatham dockyard. These buildings differed only in name from other naval storehouses and their functions were interchangeable. The southernmost of the two late eighteenth-century storehouses on Anchor Wharf, Chatham, still contains stout lattice partitions suggesting that it was probably used as a lay-apart store. Although it was convenient to site such buildings near wharves, this was not always possible, although the Chatham example and the great double quadrangle of storehouses begun at Plymouth Dock in the 1760s and partly used as lay-apart stores, came near to this ideal. The latter were destroyed by bombing (4, 87).

Present-use stores, a variant on general purpose stores, seem to have been a mid-eighteenth-century development, apparently designed to contain a wide variety of the more common items needed by a warship equipping for sea. Such buildings were generally sited in the centre of dockyards near to the main jetties and wharves, but like most dockyard stores their designations could change as quickly as their contents. Among the best remaining examples of buildings once present-use stores are the handsome 9, 10 and 11 Stores flanking the approach to *Victory* at Portsmouth.

Until well into the nineteenth century naval storehouses were largely indistinguishable from dockyard workshops in appearance so that documentary sources are essential for positive identification. The greatest concentration of storehouses of all sorts was to be found until 1942 in South Yard, Devonport. Here the Georgian planners laid out a great double quad-

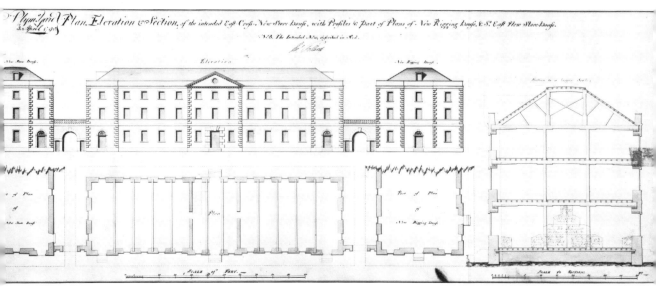

Plym Yard Plan, Elevation & Section, *of the intended East Cross New Store house, with Profiles & part of Plans of New Rigging house, & Sc East New Store house.*

N.B. The Intended Plan, described in Red.

Elevation

New Rigging house.

Plan

Part of Plan of New Rigging house

87. *Above* Roughly contemporary with 9, 10, and 11 Stores at Portsmouth were these storehouses at Plymouth. Designed to form a large double quadrangle of eight buildings, only seven were built 'plain, strong and convenient' as the Navy Board demanded in 1763. All were destroyed in air raids in 1941–2.

88. *Right* Not all naval storehouses were grand and impressive architecture. This part of the 1774 Plymouth model shows rows of simple timber-framed buildings, some used to season timber, others as masthouses and small boat workshops and stores. Beyond are the buildings of the ropery.

rangle of stone-built warehouses and workshops, in aggregate far eclipsing anything to be found elsewhere. The largest surviving individual storehouses are the two on Anchor Wharf, Chatham. Their combined lengths exceed the 1140 feet of the adjacent double ropehouse, and they owe their size and height to the lack of space for expansion elsewhere in this river yard (**90**).

Storing ships' boats demanded buildings with wider than normal doorways; three good examples of this type are grouped round the boat pond just inside the main entrance to Portsmouth Dockyard. The two single-storey timber framed and clad boathouses are nineteenth-century but are typical of their kind and could have been built at any time since the mid-seventeenth century; the larger brick building dating from 1845 is notable for its use of cast and wrought iron members to support the upper floor (**49, 50, 51**). At Chatham the long timber building north of the north mast pond is another example of this type (**52**).

89. Fire was the hazard most feared in the royal dockyards. Fireproof construction of large buildings had to await cast and wrought iron replacing timber structural members. One of the earliest fireproof buildings is this curious former pay office at Portsmouth. It may date back to the 1790s.

90. A 1793 design for the northernmost of the Anchor Wharf storehouses at Chatham (68). These were the largest storehouses ever built by the Navy Board. This one was partly used as a Fitted

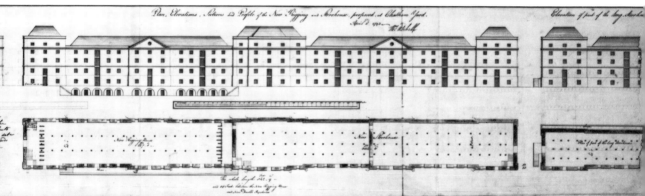

Rigging House. Here, cordage was cut to the correct lengths for each class of warship.

91. *Opposite top* Sheerness. The great Quadrangle Storehouse contracts for which were placed in 1822. It was designed by Edward Holl and was of fireproof construction. The concentration of all stores in one building, a reversion to earlier practice, was partly the result of the cramped nature of Sheerness. The building was demolished in the late 1970s.

Ships' mast timbers demanded highly specialised storage. To keep the timber supple and to prevent it drying out meant storing the fir poles under water in mast ponds. Chatham has the last such pond, excavated early in the eighteenth century. Originally, it was equipped with two parallel rows of brick arches which kept the mast timber in place under water (13).

Such was the thoroughness of the modernisations of the main dockyards in the latter part of the eighteenth century that none of these had need to augment their storage facilities significantly in the nineteenth century. When Sheerness was rebuilt in the aftermath of the Napoleonic wars, Holl and Rennie reverted to the 1690 Plymouth Dock idea of one huge central storehouse, as the dockyard was not large enough to justify a series of more specialised individual buildings. This was the first major storehouse to be designed for the dockyards after Charles Bage's pioneering iron-framed factory at Shrewsbury built in 1796–7; significantly, the Sheerness building was also of entirely fireproof construction. It was demolished in 1979.

At the overseas bases adequate warehouses were of paramount import-

92. Sheerness Boatstore, 1859. Famous in construction history as the first multi-floored metal-framed building, it is clearly derived from experience gained from earlier metal slip housings at Portsmouth and Chatham. Like 7 Slip roof at Chatham, this was designed by G. T. Green.

ance, not just for the vital reserve of stores but also, until dry-docks became available, to contain equipment from warships on careen. If, as at Minorca and Malta, suitable buildings were available when the navy first arrived, these were rented, but usually it was necessary to build or import prefabri-cated buildings.

Until the mid-nineteenth century, overseas bases were too small to jus-tify the great ranges of storebuildings to be found in most of the home dockyards. Generally, they had one or two large warehouses for the most common items likely to be needed by warships on station, in particular canvas, cordage and spars, all of which were susceptible to storms or enemy action. The smaller spars were kept inside storebuildings, the larger in spar yards.

The oldest storehouses remaining overseas are ones completed in 1774 on Saffron Island, Minorca. These are linked single-storey ranges now used by the Spanish navy. Later and larger ones, built of London stock bricks, have recently been restored at English Harbour, Antigua (110), while Bermuda has three handsome general purpose storebuildings constructed between 1857 and 1860. The largest, rivalling the home dockyards, are those built as part of the modernisation and expansion of Gibraltar dockyard at the very end of the nineteenth century.

Chapter 5

Boundaries, Houses, Churches and Schools

As government investment in the royal dockyards grew, it tended to be matched by government concern for their security. Conventional enemy attack could be countered by a series of substantial artillery defences round the principal bases. These reached their greatest extent by the 1880s and are outside the scope of this book. But more immediate and continuing worries concerned pilfering of yard materials and in wartime fear of arson. At home there was also the turbulence of the dockyard employees to be considered, much of this unruliness stemming from government inability to pay reasonable wages at regular intervals.

Early on, dockyard boundaries could be defined by nothing more substantial than a hedge and ditch, but by the end of the seventeenth century such a pleasantly casual approach to safeguarding the nation's defence establishments was no longer considered adequate. Hedges were replaced by proper walls of which early examples survive at Portsmouth (1712) and Chatham (1716). At the former dockyard the wall follows the line of an earlier ditch and palisaded defence. Just inside the main gate, widened during the 1939–45 war, stands the contemporary porter's lodge, now occupied by his lineal successors the Ministry of Defence police (93).

At Chatham, still considered the premier dockyard in the early eighteenth century, funds were available for an altogether grander scheme. When the dockyard was extended in the second decade of the century, the high brick wall sported interval towers like Roman milecastles, their

93. Portsmouth Dockyard. The Main Gate and dockyard wall completed in 1712. Inside is the former home of the yard porter. The gateway was widened in the 1939–45 war.

94. *Above* Chatham Dock-
yard. The most imposing of
all dockyard entrances, built
in 1719. The twin towers
once housed the yard
porter and boatswain. The
coat of arms is that of
George III.

95. *Above right* Chatham
Dockyard: inside the Main
Gate. On the right is the
guardhouse built in 1764
when marines took over from
civilian watchmen. Beyond
the figurehead of HMS
Wellesley is Holl's chapel
authorised in November
1805 (**114, 115**).

false machicolations giving a decidedly military air to buildings subse-
quently used only as storerooms or residences (**96**). The main gateway,
its crenel-lated parapets above the royal coat of arms, was set between
two substantial brick towers which once housed the yard porter and boatswain; no other dockyard ever had such a grandly formal entrance (**94**).

Although the main gate at Chatham has often been attributed to Vanbrugh, there is no documentary evidence linking his name with the dockyard. Contemporary buildings inside such as the terrace and sail loft
employ similar motifs, perhaps reflecting the tastes of the then commissioner or the master shipwright. The love of military detail surfaced a century and a half later when Portsmouth dockyard's boundaries were being
extended. Here, and round the former ordnance wharf, now HMS *Vernon*,
the new walls incorporated corbelled look-outs and false firing loops, while

the Haslar Gunboat Yard across the harbour went one further with a proper wall walk for sentries.

Overseas bases, perpetually short of funds and often lacking building materials, never aspired to such architectural pretensions. A hedge sufficed at Port Mahon well into the eighteenth century (14), while the surviving brick wall and modest gateway at English Harbour, Antigua are typical of the overseas dockyards (97).

Initially, the only permanent residents within the dockyard walls were the watchmen or yard porters provided with modest houses for themselves and their families by the main entrance. The yard labour force lived outside the boundaries, creating the towns of Sheerness, Portsea and Plymouth Dock, later Devonport. But by the seventeenth century it was becoming the custom to provide housing within the dockyards for the various heads of profession such as the master shipwright and master attendant. Between eight and twelve such official houses could be found in each home dockyard. Early on, these tended to be fitted in piecemeal among the storehouses and workshops, but when Plymouth Dock was laid out in the 1690s the

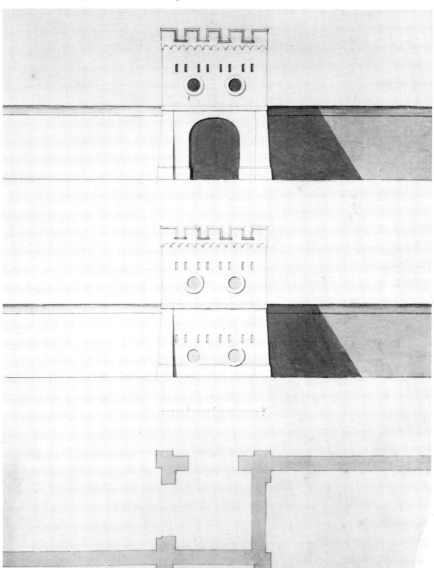

96. Chatham Dockyard. Wall towers contemporary with the Main Gate. As with the latter, ostentation not defence was uppermost in the designer's mind. Two of these delightful buildings remain in use as houses.

97. Antigua Dockyard. The eighteenth-century gateway and part of the boundary wall. Bricks for the latter were made in England. Such simple entrances were characteristic of the smaller dockyards.

officers were grouped in a magnificent terrace dominating the heart of the yard but suitably removed from the clamour of the working area (**3**).

The grandest house in the centre of the Plymouth terrace was for the commissioner of the dockyard. By then, all except the Thames yards, which were close enough to London for direct supervision, had outstationed Navy Board commissioners in day to day charge, though Sheerness was still treated as an outpost of Chatham. At the older yards the commissioners' residences had to be fitted in as best as they might, but as Plymouth was brand new it was possible for the Navy Board to give tangible expression to the importance they attached to this post. Only two of the Plymouth residences survived the 1939–45 war (**5, 98**), but the fashion set here was copied in the other main dockyards. Long Row or the Parade at Portsmouth was built between 1715 and 1719 (**100, 101**), but with only eight houses it had to be supplemented in the 1780s by Short Row providing housing for the surgeon, master ropemaker, clerk of the ropeyard and the boatswain. Chatham's officers were rehoused in the 1720s in what is arguably now the most distinguished of all such naval terraces (**102, 103**). When Sheerness was replanned after the Napoleonic wars, Holl and Rennie followed the tradition of terrace building and their two handsome ranges of housing still stand. The Sheerness terraces were the last to be built; when Pembroke was extended a few years later, pairs of semi-detached houses were favoured.

At the overseas bases only Malta had an officers' terrace. This was magnificently sited on the waterfront overlooking Dockyard Creek and was converted in 1843 from an existing range of three houses originally built for the galley captains of the Knights (111). But Malta was an exception: the first of the overseas bases to be developed on a scale to rival some of the home dockyards and consequently the first to have a substantial complement of employees. Most of the overseas establishments, especially during periods of peace in the eighteenth century, might have only a master shipwright and a storekeeper requiring housing. Such officials were provided with small detached or semi-detached dwellings, good eighteenth-century examples remaining at Rosia Bay, Gibraltar, and rather later ones at English Harbour, Antigua (110).

Early accommodation tended to be scaled strictly according to rank. The seventeenth-century housing at Chatham for example, provided a 'banqueting house' for the master shipwright, two dining rooms for the clerk of the cheque, but only a parlour for the clerk of the survey. Naturally

98. Plymouth Dockyard. The imposing terrace designed in 1692 for the commissioner and twelve senior dockyard officers. At each end were offices.

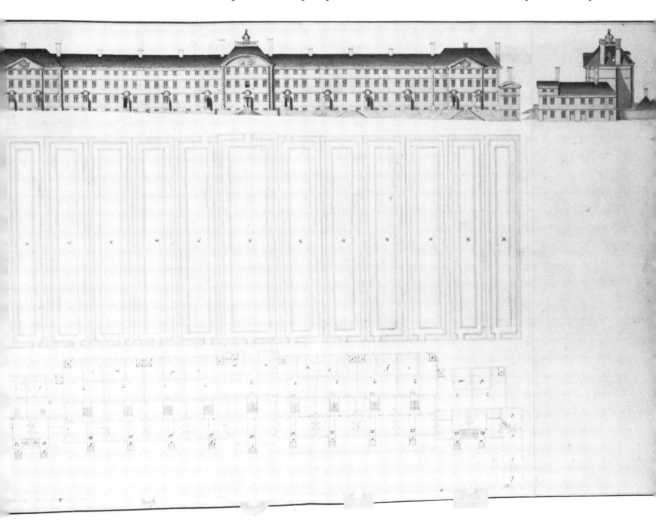

the commissioner did considerably better, having not just a banqueting house but also a fountain.

Outstationed commissioners were powerful men with accommodation to reflect their status. The existing commissioner's house at Chatham, latterly the home of the Port Admiral and known as Medway House, was built in 1703 at the express and repeated request of the incoming commissioner who had become used to the newer and grander accommodation, at

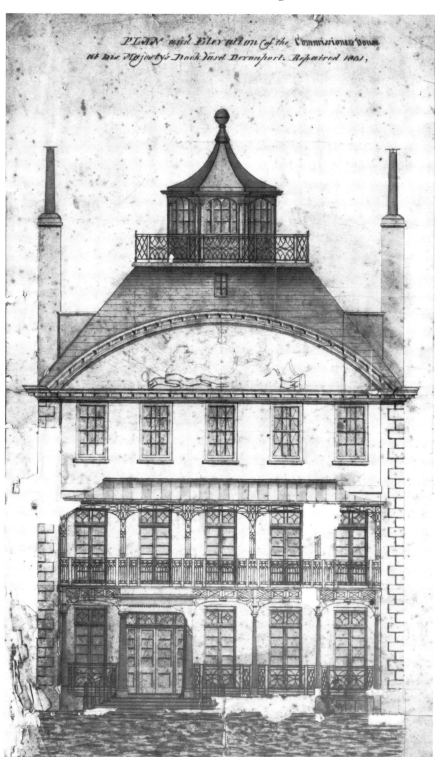

99. The Commissioner's house in 1831. By then it had acquired handsome iron balconies, while the shifting of the front door and modifications to the fenestration suggest quite substantial internal alterations.

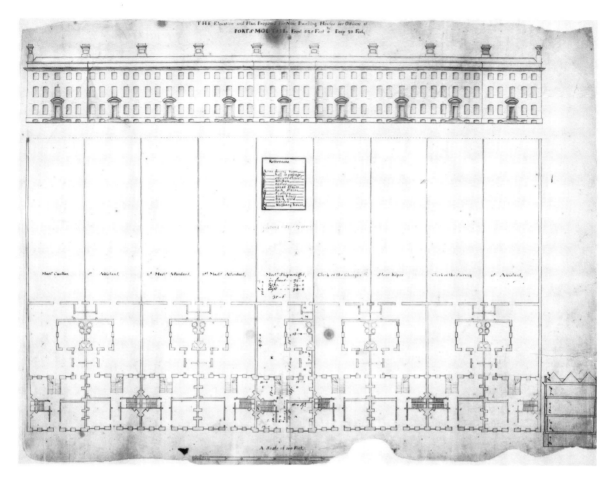

100. *Above* Completion of the Plymouth terrace was a spur to officers in other dockyards. In 1719 the eight senior officers below the Commissioner at Portsmouth were rehoused in this range, notably less grand than that at the Devon yard. The Commissioner always had a detached house at Portsmouth.

101. *Right* Portsmouth Dockyard terrace today. The front was probably rendered in 1832 but the rear elevations are still made as completed in 1719.

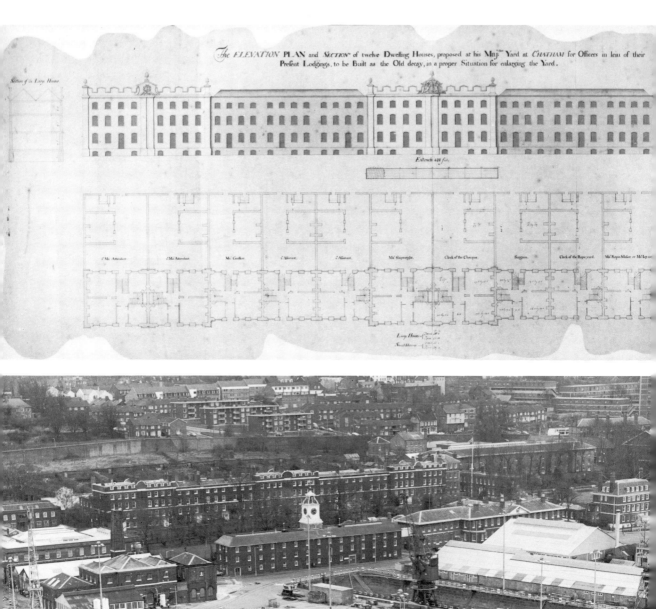

The ELEVATION PLAN and SECTION of twelve Dwelling Houses, proposed at his Maj.ties Yard at CHATHAM for Officers in lieu of their Present Lodgings, to be Built as the Old decay, in a proper Situation for enlarging the Yard.

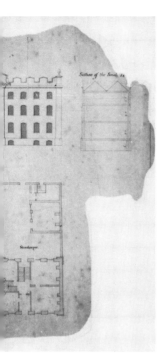

102. *Above* Chatham was the last of the 'big three' dockyards to rehouse its senior staff as part of a major expansion programme begun c. 1717. This early design for the existing terrace of twelve houses probably dates from 1721/2.

103. *Opposite* The centre of the Georgian dockyard at Chatham in May 1982. Behind the clocktower building is the officers' terrace completed in 1731. In the foreground the three dry-docks date from the 1850s; the far one was used to construct HMS *Achilles* (20). To the right is the Commissioner's House of 1703 and beyond it the Sail Loft (1723) and Chapel (1805).

Plymouth Dock. The preliminary design was quite possibly sketched out by Commissioner St Lo himself and then perhaps worked out in detail by the master shipwright at Chatham. Surprisingly, no attempt seems to have been made to relocate the house further away from the cramped centre of the dockyard and it was built on the site of its seventeenth-century predecessor. Fifteen years later when Chatham was subject to an expansion programme and the buildings in the old centre were demolished, the commissioner's house was too new for such treatment and was left in splendid isolation. The other officers were rehoused in the surviving terrace.

The Chatham commissioner's house is the oldest dockyard building remaining intact. It has been little altered and still contains its original staircases and much early panelling (104). At the head of the main staircase is the famous painted ceiling, reputedly from the Great Cabin of the *Royal Sovereign*. Executed in oils on wood, probably by Thomas Highmore, it depicts an assembly of the gods. Documentary evidence is lacking, but it could well have been installed here soon after completion of the house (105).

The grandest commissioner's house, now Admiralty House, is in Portsmouth Dockyard. Built between 1782 and 1787 to a design by Samuel Wyatt, it replaced a mid-seventeenth-century residence then considered to be in poor order and in the way of a modernisation scheme. The Surveyor to the Navy Board considered the old residence capable of repair, but he proved no match for Commissioner Martin who appears to have employed Samuel Wyatt himself, not merely to provide a report condemning the old house, but also to attach to this his plans for a new one. Wyatt's design is restrained, dignified and large. The last quality stemmed from the triple role expected here: as a family home, an office for the commissioner and, as it was Portsmouth, a residence for the monarch on his not infrequent visits to the fleet (106). It was this last which probably persuaded the Navy Board to agree to the rebuilding, though they were to find the final bill more than two and a half times greater than Wyatt's original estimate of £6,000. Such bitter medicine to a Navy Board perpetually short of money may have been made slightly more palatable by the brief romance in 1785 between Commissioner Martin's seventeen-year-old daughter and Prince William Henry, soon to be Duke of Clarence and later William IV, but then a humble lieutenant on the *Hebe*. Like its equivalent at Chatham, Admiralty House has been little altered, but while the former used to exude the cheerful atmosphere of a home, the latter, in spite of valiant efforts by a succession of occupants, remains very much as Wyatt intended it: a formal residence fit to entertain a monarch.

If the Navy Board had regrets over the eventual cost of the Portsmouth house, no such qualms should have troubled them on completion of arrangements to house a commissioner at Gibraltar. Here, with land scarce and building expensive, they rented in 1793 the new house built as a retirement home by Colonel Green of the Royal Engineers, who had played such a distinguished part in the Great Siege of 1779–1783. In 1799 they purchased the estate for £1,500. A later commissioner's wife aptly described

104. *Right* Chatham Dockyard. The Commissioner's House, begun in 1703 and now the oldest intact naval building in the country. It still contains much early panelling. It became the home of successive Port Admirals until October 1983.

105. *Opposite below* Chatham Dockyard. The famous painted ceiling at the head of the main staircase in the Commissioner's House. Probably executed by Thomas Highmore for the Great Cabin of the *Royal Sovereign*, it may have come here soon after completion of the house. Painted in oils on wood, it depicts an assembly of the gods with Mars in the centre receiving a shell crown from Neptune, a fitting subject after the victory of La Hogue.

106. *Top right* The former Commissioner's House at Portsmouth, now Admiralty House, designed by Samuel Wyatt and built between 1782 and 1787. Its cost—£15,000—could not have pleased the Navy Board but the house had to be large enough to accommodate George III on his visits to Portsmouth.

107. *Above right* Gibraltar. The former Commssioner's House, originally built by Lieutenant Colonel William Green and purchased by the Navy Board in 1796. If architecturally undistinguished, it enjoys superb views across to North Africa. It is now the flag officer's residence.

the building as 'like a good comfortable large farmhouse', a description not inappropriate today in spite of several quite extensive refurbishments. Sited in extensive grounds half-way up the Rock and with magnificent views across to North Africa, its setting was to be rivalled only by the later commissioner's house at Bermuda (**107**).

Outstationing of commissioners at the overseas bases only began in the last years of the eighteenth century, and then only at Gibraltar and later at Halifax, Malta and Bermuda, although a commissioner is mentioned at Antigua in the 1780s. Normally, the smaller yards remained in the nominal charge of a storekeeper or master shipwright, but in practice the senior naval officer on station exerted his authority, not always to the satisfaction of the Navy Board in faraway London. Such officers would usually live

108. *Above right* Antigua Dockyard. The early nineteenth-century quarters built to accommodate naval officers while their ships were being careened. Below, cisterns hold some 450 tons of fresh water.

109. *Right* Antigua. Clarence House built in the style of a plantation house for the young Duke of Clarence while he was stationed in the West Indies with Nelson in 1786.

on board their ships, unless they felt the need to secure private accommodation ashore. An exception to this was Prince William Henry's posting to the West Indies in December 1786 as captain of HMS *Pegasus*. At English Harbour, where the senior naval officer was Captain Horatio Nelson on HMS *Boreas*, Prince William was provided with a residence similar to those of island plantation owners. This still stands in its own grounds on a low bluff overlooking the tideless harbour, well positioned to catch cooling breezes and safely above what must once have been a crowded and insanitary anchorage. The principal accommodation is on one floor raised over a semi-basement which in a plantation house would have been slave quarters. The latter is built of stone, but the main part is timber-framed with timber cladding. Prince William's house, now Clarence House, was possibly provided by the Navy Board although it could have been a gift from the island legislature; it survived closure of the base in 1889 by becoming first the governor's and now the president's country residence (**109**).

In Antigua dockyard itself stands a block of residences built early in the nineteenth century on top of a great stone cistern. Their purpose was unusual: they were not for dockyard officials but for use by senior officers of a ship on careen, a reflection of one of the most important functions of an overseas base (108). Nearby is a small cookhouse for the crew whose galley fire would have had to be extinguished during such an operation.

When the Royal Navy established itself at Malta at the beginning of the nineteenth century, there was no need to build accommodation; plenty was available to rent or buy in the capital and in the three cities adjacent to Dockyard Creek. But while officials here were adapting the former dockyard of the Knights to meet British requirements, their colleagues across the Atlantic on Bermuda were faced with the far more formidable task of starting from scratch on a largely uninhabited Ireland Island. Here the prime requirement was to establish an operational base secure against possible American attack. As a consequence, Bermuda alone among overseas bases continued to have large sums of money spent on it in the fifteen or so years after the end of the Napoleonic wars.

By 1820 the nucleus of Bermuda dockyard was established and the resident commissioner felt able to press for suitable accommodation for himself. No more dramatic site could have been chosen for the new house than the area selected on the very tip of Ireland Island. Here the rocky promontory, soon to be encircled by the bastioned defences enclosing the

110. Antigua Dockyard. The Naval Officer's and Storekeeper's House. Constructed in 1855 it was one of the last major buildings erected here before the dockyard's closure on 28 June 1889. The building to the right is the late-eighteenth-century Copper and Lumber Store, the largest storehouse in the dockyard.

111. Malta. The officers' terrace overlooking Dock-yard Creek. Originally a terrace of three houses for the Knights' galley captains, it was converted into six residences between 1843 and 1846. There can surely have been few more desirable official billets.

adjacent ordnance yard and the dockyard beyond, gave the house commanding views in all directions. As both labour and materials were expensive, Edward Holl, the Navy Board's architect, had as much as possible prefabricated in London. Although he died in 1824 at an early stage in the project and all subsequent drawings are by his successor George Ledwell Taylor, there is little doubt that the basic design of the house is Holl's. It is a well proportioned two-storey building raised on a low podium with deep verandas to both floors.

Holl was already well experienced in the use of iron as a structural material, having employed it in the spinning house at Devonport ropeyard and at the sawmills and leadmill at Chatham. At Bermuda he made extensive use of cast and wrought iron for the roof framing, principal floor joists and the verandas. All these were prefabricated in London and shipped out in transports and the West India packet from Deptford along with joi-

112. Bermuda. The main elevation of the Commissioner's House, partly designed by Holl and built between 1822 and 1831. Apart from the balconies, iron was used extensively for roof members shipped, like most of the construction materials from England.

nery work, the roofing material and much of the stonework. By so doing, Holl hoped not only to lessen costs but also to thwart local commissioners with architectural aspirations of their own.

On both counts the Navy Board were doomed to disappointment. Bermuda lies several thousand miles from London and a combination of labour problems, two ambitious commissioners and a change of architect part way through sent costs spiralling well before the house was completed in 1831. The stone semi-basement, the placing of the kitchens and various other alterations were the result of local initiative, although Commissioner Lewis's attempts to have the verandas extended round to the west side were forbidden by his parent board. In this he was thwarted, not having access to a supply of cast and wrought iron to match the rest of the veranda, despite his plea that he needed a look-out on this the most likely side to see approaching American warships. If nothing else, this reason captures

113. Portsmouth. St Ann's Church built between 1785 and 1787. Inside is a three-sided gallery. After bomb damage, the west end was shortened by two bays.

something of the more leisurely warfare of the period. Ironically, the house had been completed for less than a year before the commissioners of the Navy Board were abolished. Thereafter the house had a chequered career in naval and military hands before being left derelict. It is currently being restored by the Bermuda Maritime Trust (**112**).

Gardens were notable features of nearly all the dockyard residences; like the houses themselves, they were carefully sized according to the rank of the tenant. Commissioners naturally had the largest, that round Wyatt's commissioner's house at Portsmouth being particularly notable and eclipsed in size only by that surrounding the Gibraltar residence. Chatham commissioners boasted a separate hayfield, enabling one to justify construction of a twenty-foot-square barn in 1737. Terraces all had long walled gardens to the rear, those at Chatham and Sheerness being particularly notable survivors. Post-war labour costs have meant that only flag officers are still entitled to gardening staff so that it is generally only in the former commissioners' houses now occupied by admirals that formal gardens are maintained.

Dockyard plans of the eighteenth and nineteenth centuries sometimes show small-scale plans of gardens, but planting details are rare. A tantalising glimpse into one of the gardens at Chatham is provided in a manuscript recording fruit tree planting over three seasons from 1709 to 1711. Among 29 trees planted were 'an orange apricock', a 'red Roman Nectarine', a 'yellow amidot pear', a 'Belshivereux peach', several golden pippins and a 'golden Runnett'.

For most of the eighteenth and nineteenth centuries resident officials, their families and servants together with the yard watchmen and porters probably rarely exceeded a hundred people in any one major dockyard. In the smaller overseas bases a quarter of that figure was probably the norm. For long the Navy Board did not consider the spiritual welfare of these small communities to be its concern, although chaplains had been going to sea with the fleet for centuries. The Board probably assumed that dockyard residents could attend the nearest parish church, as happened at Chatham, but this was not always easy, especially in winter, when the dockyard was far removed from the nearest centre of population.

The first move to have a chapel actually within a dockyard was made at Portsmouth in 1703 in a petition to the Lord High Admiral, Prince George of Denmark, from Commissioner William Giffard and a large number of the dockyard employees. The latter nearly all lived in Portsea, the community which had grown up to serve the dockyard and which was some way from the parish church in the older settlement of Portsmouth. Commissioner Giffard's petition was granted, but the Navy Board's involvement was limited to providing a site for the chapel. Money for its construction was raised locally and every dockyard employee had twopence a month withheld from his wages to endow a minister. At Plymouth a similar solution was adopted where there was an even more acute problem of distance from the parish centre.

No government money was spent on dockyard chapels before 1734 when additional pews and a gallery were installed at Portsmouth for pupils from the new naval academy, but by the middle of the century the Navy Board was making modest contributions to maintenance of the fabric. The first chapel to be entirely funded by the government is St Ann's at Portsmouth, begun in 1785 to replace the original which stood in the way of the dockyard modernisation scheme. A pleasantly proportioned plain brick building with a pedimented western elevation and a gallery round three sides of the interior, it clearly derives its inspiration from contemporary nonconformist chapels. Perhaps surprisingly, it was almost certainly designed by the then Surveyor to the Navy Board, Mr Marquand, rather than by the yard officers. After bomb damage to its western end, it was repaired to its present shortened plan, a reflection of the post-war decline in congregations. With the closure of Chatham chapel, St Ann's is now the sole dockyard church to remain in regular use (113).

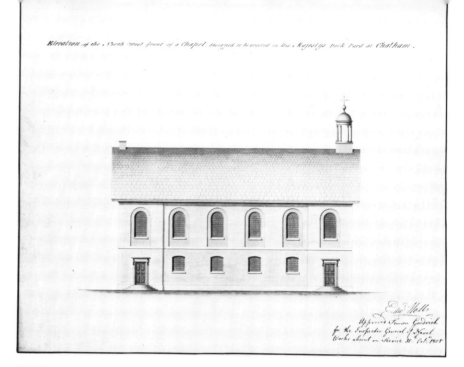

114. *Above right* Chatham. Holl's 1805 design for the dockyard chapel. Hitherto, a succession of hulks had been used for divine service. **(96)**.

115. *Right* Chatham; the interior of the chapel showing the original box pews in the gallery. Seating was strictly according to rank.

As Navy Board architect, Edward Holl was to be responsible for three chapels. In 1797 an Act of Parliament authorised a new chapel at Plymouth Dock, but it was to be late 1814 before work on it actually began; the building was destroyed in the 1939–45 war. A few years later, Holl collaborated with Rennie on a chapel for Sheerness; this rather austere building still stands, although long disused for its original purpose.

Chatham dockyard, not far from the centres of Chatham and Gillingham, had less cause to have its own place of worship, although from the latter part of the eighteenth century a succession of hulks were converted cheaply into floating chapels and moored alongside the yard. However, in November 1805 the Admiralty authorised construction of a proper chapel just inside the main gate. Also designed by Holl, it was built by the dockyard craftsmen and completed in 1810. Notable for its good proportions, its unusual Venetian-light east window and its three-sided gallery with tiered box pews partly carried on elegant fluted cast iron columns, it is arguably the most attractive of the three surviving dockyard chapels. Its last regular service was the midnight service on Christmas Eve 1981 (114, 115).

Abroad, none of the bases had purpose-built chapels for there were not the congregations to fill them before the middle of the nineteenth century. Local labour worshipped in its own communities while ex-patriates could, if they wished, attend services held by the military garrisons. Only at Malta are there references to a chapel as early as 1827, but this was almost certainly an adaption of a casemate built by the Knights.

The eighteenth-century official interest in the spiritual welfare of dockyard employees broadly coincided with moves to improve the training of sea officers for the navy. By 1700 most naval officers began their careers between the ages of twelve and fourteen by going to sea as Volunteers-per-Order. After six or seven years of practical seamanship they sat an examination which, if passed, enabled them to become third lieutenants. For their more general education during this time, they relied on the ships' chaplains. By the 1720s it was increasingly felt that such a system was too haphazard and that a more formal training of future officers would benefit the navy and the nation.

In February 1729 an Order-in-Council established the first school for potential officers; this was to be the naval academy established in Portsmouth dockyard which was to open its doors to its first intake in 1733. As the Navy Board recorded, it was designed '...for the reception and better educating and training up of forty young gentlemen for His Majesty's Service at sea, instead of the establishment now in force for volunteers on board His Majesty's ships; as also for the reception of a mathematical master, three ushers and a French master for their instruction, with proper outhouses for accommodation...'

At first the academy was not an unqualified success, for its fees, comparable to those charged by the major public schools, put it beyond the reach of many of the sons of sea officers whom the scheme was intended to help. Later, matters improved after George III endowed fifteen places for sons of sea officers, but its effect on the course of naval affairs in the eighteenth century is difficult to discern. However, its importance is that it represents a realisation by the authorities that a formal as well as a practical education could only benefit the service. In 1806 it was renamed the Royal Naval College; Dartmouth Royal Naval College is its direct descendant.

The buildings of the old Naval Academy still stand in the south-west corner of Portsmouth dockyard and are now used as the staff officers' mess.

116. *Above* Portsmouth.
The Naval Academy of
1729, now the Staff
Officers' Mess.

117. *Right* Portsmouth.
The former School for
Naval Architecture,
probably designed by Holl
in 1815.

They are built of the agreeable plum-coloured brick which is such a fea-
ture of Portsmouth and the building is notable for its handsome cupola,
a later addition. Also slightly later is a range to the rear of the H-plan
main building, probably once for accommodation for pupils. The original
designer is unknown, but indications are that he was a London architect
employed by the Navy Board. If so, this is almost certainly the first building
in Portsmouth dockyard to be designed by a professional architect (**116**).

Diagonally across from the old naval academy stands a building which
was also a pioneer in naval education. For most of the eighteenth century
it was a widely held view that French warships were better designed and
had superior sailing qualities to their English counterparts. Much of the
blame for this apparent state of affairs was held to lie with the master
shipwrights. These had risen from the ranks of shipwrights, all of whom

118. Unicorn Gate, Portsmouth, once the entrance to the Victorian dockyard but originally one of the town gates of Portsea dating from c. 1770. In the 1860s an enlightened Admiralty purchased this and the Lion Gateway, saving both from certain destruction.

had begun their careers as apprentices. Such a system undoubtedly produced skilled practical men but ones often lacking any theoretical knowledge and ignorant of technical developments elsewhere. As an 1806 commissioners' report noted, the nation's principal weapons of war were designed and built by men who had no formal training in mathematics, mechanics or marine architecture.

To help remedy this situation, the 1806 report proposed the introduction of a class of Superior Apprentices. Recruiting standards for these were to be raised and 25 were to be signed up annually and given a formal training and education. Pressure for these places was such that initially the Navy Board apparently had little difficulty in stipulating that each candidate had to provide sureties of £500 to be forfeit if he left naval service within ten years of completing his training. The proposals in this 1806 report were adopted in 1809 when George III issued an Order in Council 'for introducing a better and more skilful description of shipwright officers into His Majesty's Royal Dockyards'. Initially, pupils shared facilities at the Royal Naval College but in 1815 funds were provided for a purpose-built school. This, a pleasant two-storey pedimented building of yellow stock brick matching the commissioner's house opposite, was almost certainly designed by Edward Holl and completed in 1817. The school's output was never high and changing circumstances led to the scrapping of the course in the 1830s. An 1833 report, though, showed that many of its early pupils by then held responsible posts in all the dockyards. The building has long ceased to be used for educational purposes, but it was the ancestor of all subsequent dockyard technical schools and apprentice training centres (**117**).

Chapter 6
Provisioning the Fleet

When wind was motive power, length of time at sea was dictated ultimately by the quantity of victuals on board ship. Until the invention of canning and refrigeration in the nineteenth century the science of food preservation was rudimentary. Salt was the chief preservative, and once the limited supplies of fresh provisions had been consumed, scurvy was one of the most feared hazards of a long voyage. Inevitably, choice of provisions was limited, although by the latter part of the eighteenth century more enlightened captains were combatting scurvy with supplies of citrus fruits, while from 1782, largely at the instigation of the naval physician James Lind, sauerkraut was added to the list of official provisions specifically as an anti-scorbutic.

Nevertheless, a Royal Navy seaman in the mid-Victorian navy would have enjoyed—if that is the correct term—a diet very similar to that of his predecessor serving under Queen Anne. Biscuits, beef, pork, peas, fish, butter, cheese and beer were staple foods. Oatmeal, sugar, soup concentrate and sauerkraut had been added in the eighteenth century while on the West Indies station cocoa was first provided in the 1780s. Abroad, if local purchases were possible, captains often substituted wine for beer, while raisins, rice and olives added variety. The monotony of this range was compounded by the very limited means of preparing and cooking food at sea. The system of messing did not necessarily encourage any latent

119. Cooperage buildings of 1766 in the former Weevil Victualling Yard, Gosport. This photograph was taken in 1970 when the official issue of naval rum was ended, ending also the craft of the cooper in the royal dockyards. Before canning and refrigeration, coopers were vital to all victualling establishments.

120. The grand entrance to the Royal William Victualling Yard, Stonehouse, designed by John Rennie and built between 1824 and 1832.

culinary talents among mess members, while even after the introduction of Brodie's firehearths in the second half of the eighteenth century, pressure on ships' galleys was such as to exclude virtually everything except the ubiquitous stew. Seamen, however, were conservative in their tastes: new types of provisions tended to be regarded with suspicion if not hostility; what they wanted above all were familiar foods of good quality and ample quantity.

Feeding the fleet was the responsibility of the Victualling Board, an organisation which remained virtually unchanged from the end of James II's reign to its absorption by the Admiralty in 1832. Its first headquarters was on Tower Hill where a bakery and storehouse had been established in the reign of Queen Elizabeth I. In 1742 expansion dictated a move downriver to Deptford which was to remain headquarters of naval victualling for over 200 years. For the last century of its life here the premises were known as the Royal Victoria Victualling Yard; two fine ranges of late eighteenth-century rum warehouses, the officers' terrace and the former yard

121. The heart of the Royal William Victualling Yard is the basin flanked by the flour mill/bakery, seen on the left and the brewery (122). In the centre is the quadrangular Melville Square Storehouse, begun in 1829.

gateway are virtually all that survive today. In its heyday though, Deptford was well sited to buy supplies from the London food markets and to act as depot for Woolwich, Harwich, Sheerness, Chatham and ships at the Nore. If the dockyards themselves were for long the industrial centres of England, the Victualling Office was the country's first really large-scale food manufacturing and catering organisation, preceding rivals in this field by several centuries.

At Deptford much of the work was concerned with appointing and overseeing agents and contractors. These men either supplied provisions such as grain or butter direct to the victualling yards or were chandlers at ports frequented by warships. Except at some of the overseas stations, chandlers would not normally expect to provision vessels for long voyages. Their task was to meet urgent or unexpected needs and to maintain supplies of fresh foods to any warships based in their vicinity. Major provisioning took place at or near the principal fleet bases where the Victualling Office created its own establishments. These varied in size and importance depending on their location and whether they manufactured as well as stored food and drink. In the latter part of the seventeenth century when Chatham had its heyday as a fleet base, its victualling premises were scenes of great activity. In 1691 the slaughterhouse could process 45 bullocks a week, but on the whole it was found more convenient to provision warships at Sheerness or at Blackstakes at the mouth of the Thames where

122. Rennie's brewery at Royal William Yard. Like the bakery part was carried forward to the wharf edge to enable vessels to be unloaded directly into the building.

barges could come direct from London. As a consequence, victualling premises remained small at Chatham and were mostly rented buildings. The depot was finally closed in 1822 in favour of a new yard at Sheerness; nothing remains today.

As the south coast dockyards grew in importance, so did their victualling premises. Although some supplies always came from the London food markets, bulk processing of meat, drink, bread and biscuits was more conveniently done locally. Portsmouth and Plymouth joined Deptford as manufacturing centres supplying not only the home fleet but also victualling depots overseas at Gibraltar, Minorca and in the West Indies. In the nineteenth century further yards were to be established at Malta, Bermuda and Ascension Island. Of these Malta was the most important, with its own mill and bakery constructed in the mid 1840s, but Minorca and Malta a century before made their own contribution to naval life with their gin and rum distilleries. To this day, nearly two centuries after the Royal Navy ceased using Port Mahon, small distilleries in the town produce gin to much the same specification as that obtainable by George III's seamen.

In common with its sister boards, the Victualling Office was usually short of funds, but whereas dockyard and ordnance operations dictated heavy expenditure on creation of secure establishments, there was much less pressure on the Victualling Board to do likewise. Its buildings, frequently rented or leased, were often scattered in the dockyard towns, their siting dictated as much by local markets and mills as by convenience to the water-front and fleet anchorage. In the 1780s, comparatively large sums were spent on redeveloping facilities at Deptford, but not until after the Napoleonic wars were large sums of money available to create centralised and architecturally notable victualling yards at Portsmouth and Plymouth, rivalling the best developments of the Board of Ordnance and Navy Board.

Given this comparatively late development of adequately-sized and well-planned victualling yards, it is perhaps surprising that the Victualling Board managed as well as it did from its assortment of premises during the numerous wars of the eighteenth century. Unlike the Board of Ordnance, which only had to replenish warships after an engagement or when powder was found to be past its best, the Victualling Board had to sustain the navy throughout the year. If quality of victuals was the subject of frequent complaint, this was more to do with limitations in the science of food preservation than with conscious failings on the part of the Board. Sailors might die of scurvy from a vitamin deficiency, but except in unforeseen circumstances such as shipwreck, eighteenth-century British sailors did not die of starvation as a result of incompetence or negligence on the

123. Part of the interior of Melville Square showing Rennie's use of cast-iron for columns where its compressive strength was especially useful.

part of the Victualling Board. This is a remarkable record in view of the number of mouths to feed—for example, between 1774 and 1783 the number of men on sea pay rose from 17,731 to 107,446 and the latter figure was comfortably exceeded during the Napoleonic wars.

In some ways transition from a peace to a war establishment was easier for the Victualling Board than for its sisters. By the eighteenth century the London food markets were sufficiently well-developed to be able to cope with a surge of purchasing for the navy and barrel supplies—essential for storage purposes—do not seem to have been a particular problem; while distribution to fleet bases was a matter of hiring extra merchant vessels. The major problem tended to be storage for these extra supplies; some would obviously go straight to warships but reserves had to be accumulated ashore. Within a year of the outbreak of the War of Spanish Succession in 1702, warehouses at Portsmouth were so full that the Board had to hire ships as floating victualling stores.

Attempts to modernise facilities in the eighteenth century tended to be spasmodic and piecemeal. By 1749 victualling operations at Chatham were mainly confined to supplying crews of guardships and those few people posted on board ships in ordinary. There was a slight growth of activity during the Napoleonic wars, but a survey in 1821 just before victualling operations were terminated here, showed that the only property actually owned by the Board was one old storehouse in Rochester. Everything else was rented from a variety of owners. After 1822, supplies at Chatham were kept on the guard ships and sheer hulks.

In the early eighteenth century, victualling operations at the Hampshire base took place on both sides of Portsmouth Harbour. In Portsmouth itself there was a large bakery and a handsome pedimented storehouse in King Street, a slaughterhouse near the Sally Port and a small wharf next to the ordnance yard. Nearby was a cornmill and a cooperage, while in 1779 the Square Tower, built as part of the Tudor defences, was acquired from the Board of Ordnance and became a meat store. On the Gosport side of the harbour good supplies of fresh spring water enabled the Board to establish a brewery which by 1716 included a brewhouse, cooperage and house for the brewer. A windmill was used to pump water to cisterns at the top of the brewhouse. In 1766 the Board centralised barrel making at Gosport and built a new cooperage. This was an irregular quadrangle of single-storey brick and timber buildings with the central area used to store barrels. Canning and refrigeration dramatically reduced the need for these, but the cooperage remained in limited production until the abolition of the naval rum issue in 1970. Its buildings are all that survive from the eighteenth century (119).

At Plymouth, where the Victualling Board had agents long before the dockyard was established in the 1690s, there was much the same pattern of development. The new dockyard created a new town, Plymouth Dock, but the Victualling Board preferred to base its operations in Plymouth. Here in the eighteenth century they had a variety of premises, including

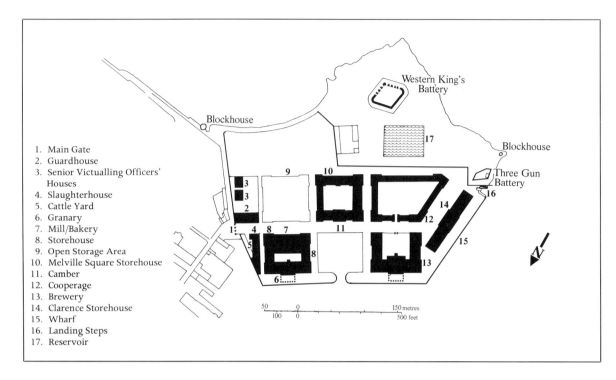

1. Main Gate
2. Guardhouse
3. Senior Victualling Officers' Houses
4. Slaughterhouse
5. Cattle Yard
6. Granary
7. Mill/Bakery
8. Storehouse
9. Open Storage Area
10. Melville Square Storehouse
11. Camber
12. Cooperage
13. Brewery
14. Clarence Storehouse
15. Wharf
16. Landing Steps
17. Reservoir

Fig. 7. Royal William Victualling Yard c. 1830.

a brewery. Many of these were leased, including the flour mills which were owned by Plymouth corporation, but such arrangements came under increasing strain during the wars at the end of the century. Geographical location made Plymouth an obvious victualling station for fleets and squadrons operating in the Atlantic and Western Approaches, but in addition it became supply point for Gibraltar, Minorca and later Ascension Island. In the later stages of the Napoleonic wars it supplied both ordnance and victuals to Wellington's Peninsular army.

After 1815 there was the inevitable post-war retrenchment in government defence spending. All available Navy Board funds were devoted to rebuilding Sheerness and the establishment of Bermuda dockyard and it was not until 1821 that the Victualling Board were in a position to modernise their own operations. They started at Plymouth where the need was greatest. In 1822 land on the Cremill peninsula was chosen for a centralised and enlarged victualling establishment. As the Victualling Board had neither experience nor staff for a construction project of this magnitude, the Navy Board undertook the building and engineering works. At that time the engineer John Rennie the younger was busy completing for the Navy Board the huge breakwater in Plymouth Sound which had been started under his father's direction. This was rightly considered one of the civil engineering wonders of the day, so it was in many ways a natural choice that Rennie, still only 29, should be asked to be responsible for the design and construction of the new victualling yard.

By the middle of 1824 all necessary land transactions had been completed

120

125. Royal William Yard. Houses for the senior victualling officers.

124. *Opposite foot* Royal William Yard. One of the simple and elegant granite staircases to the main offices.

and by early the following year Rennie had finalised his outline plans. In the Parliamentary estimates for 1825 a sum of £291,512 was allocated. This was to cover a tidal basin, wharves, a brewery, flour mill, bakery, cooperage, landing shed, slaughterhouse, quadrangle storehouse, five houses for senior officers, porters' lodge, offices, boundary walls, drains, cranes and two reservoirs. As well as being responsible for the design and execution of all civil engineering and architectural works, Rennie was also responsible for much of the machinery in the mill, brewery and bakery. It was a formidable undertaking for one man.

The Cremill peninsula forms a short rocky promontory jutting into the estuary of the Tamar where the latter joins Plymouth Sound. No building work could start until thousands of tons of rock had been blasted and quarried away to form a level area of some fourteen acres on the sheltered northern side. This took two years and included construction of a large reservoir cut into the remaining high ground. Contracts for the first building, Clarence Wharf storehouse, were let in November 1827. The contractor for this and all subsequent work here was the firm of Hugh McIntosh, also to be responsible for rebuilding the Gosport victualling yard. In 1828 work began on the brewery, boundary walls and excavation of the central basin for the lighters. In 1829 the only major new project was the quadrangle storehouse, fronting the south side of the basin and focal point of the yard. In 1830 contracts were signed for the entrance gateway, guard house, slaughterhouse, cattle yard and beef and vegetable store. In 1830 Rennie finalised plans for the huge granary mill and bakery sited on the east side of the basin opposite the brewery and work also began on plans for the officers' houses. By May 1831 work was sufficiently advanced for the Vic-

121

tualling Board to order the sale of the old premises in Plymouth and by October they were able to dispense with the rented flour mills. Even so, by January 1832 £42,000 of work was still outstanding and only the brewery was fully operational. By the end of the year the establishment was complete and named the Royal William Victualling Yard after the king. A century and a half later, Rennie's design is still intact and one of the most important groups of industrial buildings in the country (**120–124**).

Construction was in Devonian limestone with granite detailing. Inside buildings, Rennie made extensive use of cast and wrought iron for columns, principal joists and for roof members, while roofs were slate covered with copper bonnets. The whole was on a monumental scale, no more evident than when seen from the main gateway surmounted by the more than twice life-size statue of William IV. Beyond stretches the main axis of the yard, to the left the vast quadrangular Melville Square storehouse surmounted by a clocktower and named after the second Lord Melville, First Lord of the Admiralty from 1812 to 1827. Beyond it, the coopers once plied their trade in an irregular four-sided range of buildings which present largely blank façades to the outside world. To the right is the bakery and flour mill and beyond it the brewery; the view from the main gateway is terminated by Clarence storehouse. Tucked round the corner from the main gateway away from the noise and bustle of the yard, Rennie sited houses for the senior victualling staff. These overlooked what was once an open storage area but is now a pleasant expanse of lawns and trees (**125**).

The finest way to approach Royal William Yard is by boat for the tidal basin in the centre has always been the focal point and it was round this that the three principal buildings were grouped. Originally, most supplies arrived by water—both granary and brewery are carefully sited at wharf edges to enable supply vessels to be off-loaded straight into them—and all produce left in victualling lighters which transshipped their supplies into warships anchored in the Hamoaze or in Plymouth Sound.

If redevelopment had been urgent at Plymouth, it was scarcely less so at Portsmouth. At Weevil Yard on the Gosport side, the brewery had been extended during the Napoleonic wars and was able to produce 60 tons of beer daily, enough for 15,120 men, but little else had been done apart from a modernisation of the old King Street storehouse in Portsmouth. In 1812 Bentham had suggested concentrating facilities on the Gosport side but the suggestion came to nothing. In October 1824, using Plymouth as a precedent, the Victualling Board revived the idea but the Admiralty vetoed it on grounds of vulnerability and a reluctance to have the victualling officer on the opposite side of the harbour from the admiral and transport agent. There matters might have remained but for the appointment in 1827 of the Duke of Clarence as Lord High Admiral. The Duke, who had been on the West Indies station in the mid 1780s with the young Nelson, was keenly interested in naval affairs and the Victualling Board papers suggest that it was his personal enthusiasm that led to a decision in December 1827 to expand the Weevil Yard and dispose of facilities in Portsmouth.

126. Between 1828 and 1832 the old Weevil Yard at Gosport was extended, modernised and renamed Royal Clarence Victualling Yard after the Duke of Clarence, Lord High Admiral. The main entrance from the inside.

As Weevil Yard already contained an adequate cooperage and a new brewery, the principal need was for storehouses, a reservoir, a cornmill and a bakery. Houses for the senior victualling officers, wharves, new cranes and dredging the harbour pushed the estimated cost to £227,480. In the event, the final bill was probably under £200,000. The Navy Board architect, G. L. Taylor, was responsible for the design and the work was carried out by Hugh McIntosh. Land lying north of the existing yard was acquired from the Board of Ordnance and work began in the second half of 1828. As at Plymouth, Rennie was responsible for the design and supply of an engine and machinery for the mill and bakery. Work proceeded fairly rapidly and the project was completed by the end of 1832. On July 1st 1831 the name Weevil Yard was dropped in favour of the Royal Clarence Victualling Yard, a fitting tribute to William IV who had done so much to ensure its establishment.

As Clarence Yard was an amalgam of old and new, it never achieved the monumental quality of its Devon contemporary and much of Taylor's work was destroyed in wartime bombing. What survives, though, shows him to have been an architect well-versed in the best industrial building techniques of his day. Each victualling yard reflects its location in choice of building materials: where Rennie used stone, Taylor used local warm red brick with detailings in Portland stone. Like Rennie, he made extensive use of cast and wrought iron as structural material.

The landward approach to the Gosport yard is still along Weevil Lane which skirts the back of the Cooperage Green buildings before arriving at Taylor's main gateway (126). This, the guard house and the two residences

127. Royal Clarence Victualling Yard in 1898. Prominent is the mill/bakery building with its row of chimneys. In the right foreground is the slaughterhouse, while to the left lies the brewery complex extensively damaged in the 1939–45 war.

immediately inside are all stuccoed and have an agreeable Regency air. The arched gateway is a more humble version of the Plymouth one and makes do with a royal coat-of-arms instead of being capped with a statue of the sailor king. The centre of Clarence Yard was largely destroyed by enemy action (127) but on the waterfront and still a notable local landmark is Taylor's great granary and bakery (128). As at Plymouth, the granary is brought forward to the wharf edge to enable grain boats to unload directly; to minimise obstructions on the wharf, the upper floors are supported on massive cast iron columns. Except for the brackets which once carried line shafts, no trace remains within of the milling arrangements or of the steam engine to the rear. The southern wing, used as a storehouse, was bombed, but the matching northern wing is intact. Here was the spacious two-storey bakery, once equipped with Rennie's steam-driven mixing machinery. Batches of bread and biscuits were baked in nine vast circular brick-vaulted ovens set into the rear wall of the mixing room. Although long disused, these ovens remain intact. Behind the bakery are the cattle pens and cattle yards while down by the wharf edge is the former slaughter-house, a reminder of the days when the navy's meat rations arrived on the hoof from the Midlands and the west country and left in barrels packed with salt.

The introduction of canned, frozen and de-hydrated foods prepared in

124

128. Taylor's handsome mill/bakery in 1969.

specialist food factories has removed one of the major tasks of the naval victualling yards which are now just storage, distribution and administrative centres. The only sound likely to be heard at Gosport and Plymouth is the quiet hum of refrigeration machinery and it is sometimes difficult to visualise these yards in their heyday with the smell of baking and brewing, the lowing of cattle and the ringing of hammers in the cooperages.

Deptford, Portsmouth and Plymouth as manufacturing yards were a class

129. Gibraltar Victualling Yard, sole survivor of Georgian overseas victualling establishments. It comprised a house for the agent victualler and the great vaulted storehouse begun in 1807. Water was carefully channelled from the roofs of the latter to a vast underground storage tank.

apart, their victuals not just for distribution to warships in their immediate vicinity. An important aspect of their work was the supply of preserved foods to foreign stations and the smaller home dockyards such as Sheerness. At these the Victualling Office would have a number of storehouses and usually a small cooperage for the repair of damaged barrels. A storekeeper or agent would be in charge with authority to make local purchases if necessary. Nothing remains of these satellite yards in Britain, but two good examples can be seen at Gibraltar and Bermuda, the former still in use.

Gibraltar's importance as a victualling base was not fully appreciated until the very end of the eighteenth century. Until then, the Victualling Board had been content with a storehouse next to the Waterport and with accommodation in part of the White Convent. The port of Leghorn was principal supply base but its fall in June 1796, together with Napoleon's advance down Italy, caused serious problems to Jervis's fleet. Coincidentally, at Gibraltar the Victualling Board had to vacate their main storehouse which stood in the way of new defence works. At the suggestion of Lord St Vincent new premises were sited away from the town adjacent to Rosia Bay. The bay was large enough for most vessels and beyond the effective range of artillery on the Spanish mainland, while a rocky outcrop gave a measure of protection from seaward bombardment. Part of the scheme involved construction of a huge underground reservoir to store water from the rainy season. Work began on this in 1799 with most of the million bricks needed for the lining probably having to be shipped from England. The reservoir was completed by 1806 and in July the following year the Navy Board authorised a new storehouse.

The storehouse reflected its front-line position in one of the world's most powerful natural fortresses. Designed by a group of local naval and military officers and built by John Maria Boschetti, a Gibraltarian contractor, the victualling storehouse was modelled on contemporary powder magazines, but was considerably larger and was designed to withstand bombardment (**129**). 190 feet by 160 feet externally, it contained eleven vaulted rooms on each of two floors. On the first floor the vaults were supported by stone pillars with sockets for temporary partitions (**130**). The ground floor was arranged as a series of tunnel vaults linked by a single vaulted cross passage mid-way along. Walls were stone but the vaults were brick. Water from the roof was carefully channelled to the adjacent reservoir. Outside was a small courtyard with an office for the Agent Victualler, approached from Rosia Bay by an archway still bearing the legend G.I I I D G M B & H R &.

Initially, Gibraltar victualling depot would have received all its bulk supplies from England, supplementing these with fresh foods from North Africa and, when the political situation allowed, from Spain. But later in the nineteenth century it may well have been supplied from Malta for on the latter island in the 1840s the Admiralty had a bakery constructed rivalling the output of those at the home bases. Facilities inherited from the Knights included a bakery in Valletta, but with the mid-century growth

130. Part of the first floor interior of the Gibraltar storehouse.

131. From the mid-nine-
teenth century, the
Mediterranean Fleet was
supplied with bread and
biscuits from this mill/
bakery at Dockyard Creek,
Malta.

of a permanent Mediterranean fleet new premises were needed. Between 1840 and 1846 a flour mill and bakery were built alongside Dockyard Creek near San Lorenzo landing place. The architect was William Scamp, until 1841 assistant engineer to the Works Department in Woolwich Dockyard. 'Scamp's Palace' built of the local stone has dominated this part of the waterfront since although it was last used for its original purpose in the 1950s. At the southern end of the building there were once twelve great circular ovens arranged in groups of three (**131**).

The last substantial victualling depot to be built was at Bermuda in the 1850s. The first one had been proposed here in 1818, but an estimate of £65,000 caused it to be shelved in favour of a succession of storeships. A site for the victualling yard, however, was earmarked in the centre of the fortified dockyard to the north of the camber where it seems some buildings were constructed. But not until the mid 1850s was the site taken in hand and a regular victualling yard laid out. Six residences were constructed facing the camber and behind them, enclosed by a wall, were placed two storehouses. All were built of local stone, but as a concession to the climate the residences were given deep and shady verandas. After a period of dereliction in the 1950s the complex is now gradually being restored (**26**).

128

Chapter 7
Arming the Warships

Until its abolition in May 1855, the Board of Ordnance, a separate government department, was responsible for the armament of warships. Apart from some small arms and ammunition for use in emergency by the marine guards, royal dockyards normally contained no weapons. Instead, the Board of Ordnance established its own yards and powder magazines adjacent to the main fleet bases and from these supplied warships with everything from heavy guns and their equipment such as rammers, mops, sponges and quills, to the cutlasses and boarding pikes used in close engagements of the period. A warship preparing for sea would lie off the ordnance yard after leaving dockyard hands, and hoist aboard the appropriate weapons and their ammunition. On return from active service for repair or for being placed in reserve, the ordnance yard was frequently the first port of call.

Like the Navy Board, the Board of Ordnance had its headquarters in London. Its primary role was as a purchasing department, but it also had some manufacturing capacity. In the seventeenth century it produced bronze guns at its Moorfields works, while in 1717 it began gunfounding at Woolwich. These works however only supplemented production by private gunfounders, in the same way as did the gunpowder works at Faversham in Kent acquired in 1760 and those at Waltham Abbey in Essex bought some years later. For long the Tower of London was the principal arsenal, maintaining reserves of munitions for the army and navy. In the 1670s this was supplemented by Upnor Castle on the Medway just downstream from Chatham dockyard (138), and a century later by the huge group of powder magazines on the Thames at Purfleet (134). These were the chief depots for ordnance yards supplying Chatham, Portsmouth and Plymouth Dock.

Ordnance yards adjacent to dockyards chiefly needed extensive warehouses for wooden gun carriages, gunners' equipment and the various hand weapons. Limited carriage manufacture as well as normal maintenance and repairs was also undertaken, requiring a series of small workshops for armourers, smiths, carpenters, coopers and painters. As in the dockyards, senior officers were provided with housing. Ordnance yards were small compared to dockyards. However, like the latter, they needed to expand during the eighteenth and early nineteenth centuries to keep pace with the demands of the fleet. As bases were established overseas, ordnance depots were laid out in close proximity, but these generally consisted only of a

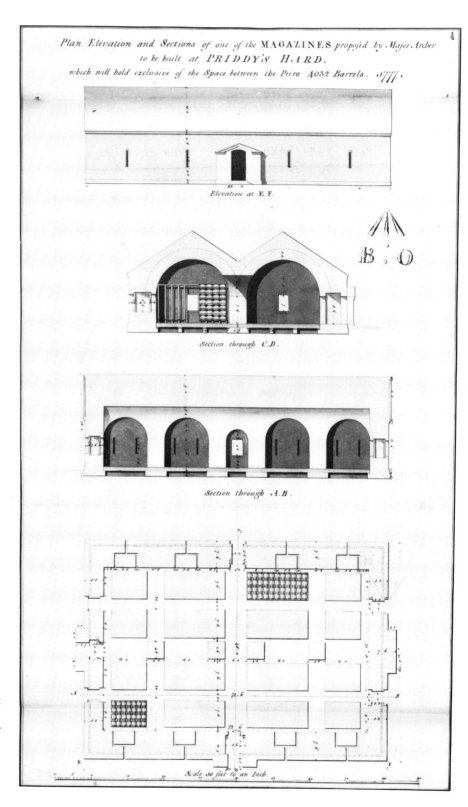

Plan Elevation and Sections of one of the MAGAZINES proposed by Major Archer to be built at PRIDDY'S HARD. which will hold exclusive of the Space between the Piers 4032 Barrels. 1777.

Elevation at E.F.

B. O

Section through C.D.

Section through A.B.

Scale 30 feet to an Inch.

132. 1777 design for a pair of gunpowder magazines at Priddy's Hard, Alverstoke. Each was to hold 4,032 barrels. Neither was built but they are very similar to the existing magazine of 1770 (plate 136).

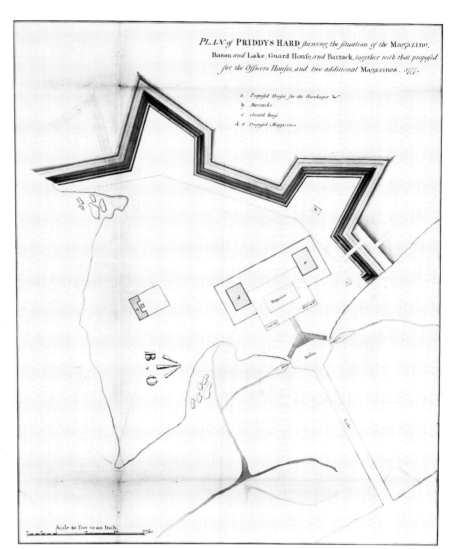

133. Priddy's Hard, Alverstoke, showing the two proposed magazines (d and e). The rest of this complex laid out in 1770 remains today much as shown here. From it, warships at Portsmouth drew their powder supplies.

powder magazine, shifting house, a room for repacking powder barrels and a yard for storing solid shot.

A central part of the Board of Ordnance's activity was ensuring supplies of gunpowder. From its own and from private works scattered across southeast England at such places as Chilworth in Surrey and Battle in Sussex, the barrels of gunpowder were sent to the main ordnance depots. Careful handling and storage were essential for apart from the obvious dangers of explosion, gunpowder needed to be kept dry and cool to preserve its power. Powder long in a barrel, especially in the often far from ideal conditions prevailing in warships' magazines, settled and caked. This was no minor problem: if records are to be believed, the Royal Navy returned some 327,750 barrels of powder as 'unfit' between January 1785 and August 1810, representing over 50 per cent of official powder production during that period. Such powder had to be carefully sifted, mixed and

134. *Above right* The great ranges of powder magazines at Purfleet on the Essex bank of the Thames. From these mid-eighteenth-century buildings transports supplied the smaller magazines at the main fleet bases. A photograph taken in 1973 shortly before partial demolition.

135. *Right* Inside one of the Purfleet magazines. Walls were double skinned and no iron was used in the construction. Note the overhead travelling crane.

repacked in special buildings adjacent to the magazines.

Even with the more cavalier approach of our forefathers to matters of safety, proper storage of gunpowder clearly needed specialised buildings. By the eighteenth century, a modern ordnance depot powder magazine was usually a rectangular brick or stone barrel-vaulted building, with double skin walls and a raised wooden floor to combat damp and ensure good ventilation. Floor boards were dowelled, while doors, shutters and window frames were copper-sheathed. Hinges, locks, handles and ventilation grills were similarly made of non-ferrous metal to reduce the danger of sparks. Above the barrel vault would be a pitched roof, the space between roof and vault sometimes filled with sand if there was considered to be a danger of enemy bombardment, while the outside walls usually needed heavy buttresses to support this load and resist the thrust of the vault.

Wherever possible, natural lighting was used inside powder magazines. When lamps were necessary, they were kept behind a thick glass panel which was approached from outside by its own lighting passage. Inside the magazine powder barrels were stacked in bays separated by partitions of heavy studding. In the nineteenth century handling of barrels was sometimes aided by a wooden travelling hand-crane running the length of the interior below the apex of the vault.

Probably the earliest relatively unaltered magazines to survive are a pair at Tilbury Fort on the north bank of the Thames. These were built in 1716 and were calculated to hold a total of 7,200 barrels, each containing some 90 pounds of powder. On the Medway the Board of Ordnance had saved money by adapting Upnor Castle in 1668 as a magazine, a role it fulfilled until 1827, while at Portsmouth the Board similarly relied heavily on the storage capacity of Square Tower at the end of Portsmouth High Street. Built in the 1490s as part of the local defences, its thick walls were ideal as secure storage, but a serious fire in the dockyard in 1760 gave the more nervous citizens cause for concern lest a similar mishap occur near the magazine. A petition to George III prayed that the powder be stored elsewhere. This was answered by the establishment of a depot up-harbour at Priddy's Hard in the 1770s.

Between 1719 and 1724 the Board of Ordnance laid out a new yard to supply the navy at Plymouth. Known as Morice Yard after the local landowner, this remains much as completed. From the start it had a small magazine on the waterfront, but this has since been demolished. By the 1740s this was proving far from adequate and much of the fleet's powder was having to be stored in Plymouth Citadel. The latter arrangement was neither convenient nor safe, for all the barrels had to be manhandled through the narrow streets of the town, while in Morice Yard itself, extra powder had to be kept in general storehouses. Worse, as Horneck the resident Board of Ordnance Surveyor reported in 1743 '. . . the common berths for merchant ship's and small vessels is generally in front of the gunwharf . . . and when the ship's company are saluting, rejoicing and firing their guns, the very flashes come ashore to the magazine without any regard being paid to its being open or shut'. The solution to these alarming states of affairs was construction of a second powder magazine which still stands. Incorporating most of the by then standard features of such buildings, it was embellished by a somewhat quirky and out of proportion brick pediment on shallow pilasters on its main elevation. Within this were placed the arms of the Duke of Montagu, Master General of Ordnance 1739–49 (**140**).

As well as being the earliest surviving magazine remaining in a naval

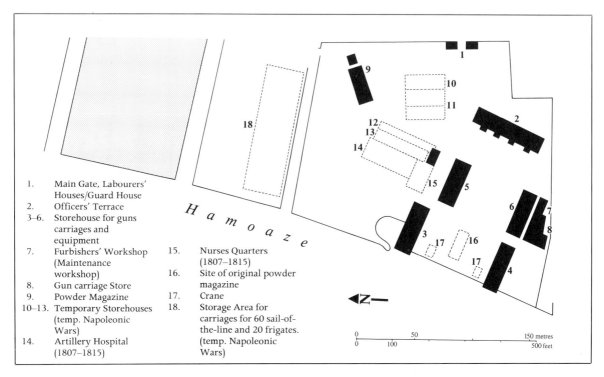

1. Main Gate, Labourers' Houses/Guard House
2. Officers' Terrace
3–6. Storehouse for guns carriages and equipment
7. Furbishers' Workshop (Maintenance workshop)
8. Gun carriage Store
9. Powder Magazine
10–13. Temporary Storehouses (temp. Napoleonic Wars)
14. Artillery Hospital (1807–1815)
15. Nurses Quarters (1807–1815)
16. Site of original powder magazine
17. Crane
18. Storage Area for carriages for 60 sail-of-the-line and 20 frigates. (temp. Napoleonic Wars)

Fig. 8. Morice Ordnance Yard, Devonport. This is now the sole intact ordnance yard of eighteenth-century date.

136. *Right* The 1770 powder magazine at Priddy's Hard, now a museum of the history of naval ordnance.

137. *Below right* The tiny basin at Priddy's Hard. From here, ammunition lighters supplied warships riding in the main channel.

ordnance yard, the Morice Yard example was also one of the last to be built within the confines of such an establishment. When additional ones were required later in the eighteenth century, both the Admiralty Board, fearful for its warships, and local citizens concerned with their own safety, united to ensure that gunpowder storage was divorced from the ordnance yards and located as far as possible from the main fleet anchorages and heavily populated areas. To achieve both requirements without impairing operational efficiency was not always easy as the Board of Ordnance found in 1766 when it proposed a powder depot on the west side of Portsmouth Harbour at Priddy's Hard. Although nobody lived nearby, the Admiralty felt that it was unduly close to the main harbour anchorage and to the victualling facilities at Weevil Yard so would consent to only one out of the three proposed magazines.

Priddy's Hard was laid out by 1773 to a design by a Captain Archer, centred on the great magazine for around 4,500 barrels of powder (**136**). This brick building stands in its own walled courtyard with a cooperage and shifting house and beyond, a small basin for the ammunition hoys (**137**). Nearby is the former house of the ordnance storekeeper, only survivor of a scheme a few years later to extend the depot and add the two magazines as first proposed. Today, Priddy's Hard lies in the heart of a Royal Navy armaments depot, its buildings housing an ordnance museum. It is not only the most complete example of its type remaining in England, but is the pioneer example of the separation of explosives away from the main ordnance yards. Its example was to be followed at Plymouth in the 1770s when magazines were built further up the Tamar at Keyham, convenient both for the fleet and for the government powder mills at St Budeaux.

Siting extra facilities at the Hampshire base to cope with the unprecedented demands of the Napoleonic wars was to cause great difficulties. In Portsmouth Harbour a series of hulks was pressed into service as floating magazines, their positions potentially far more hazardous to the fleet than would have been the full complement of three magazines proposed at Priddy's Hard. A whole new set of magazines was laid out at Marchwood on the shores of Southampton Water for both army and navy. Here, as bombardment was not considered so likely, the magazines were built without the characteristic brick vaults. Instead, massive earth banks or traverses separated each building to limit the effects of any explosion. Such banks, widely employed in gunpowder works, were to become standard features within most subsequent explosive depots. At Marchwood, small canals criss-crossed the site to provide water in case of fire. Where possible attack was expected, vaulted magazines continued to be built late into the nineteenth century. Good examples, although recently damaged, remain at Tipner on the north-west corner of Portsea Island and at Priddy's Hard itself where a large vaulted magazine complete with surrounding blast banks was built in the 1870s. At Bull Point on the Tamar is the largest such nineteenth-century establishment, little altered since completion (**143**).

Priddy's Hard was paralleled by similar establishments at overseas naval stations. Further up the harbour from Antigua dockyard stands a powder magazine of similar size, but the most impressive set are those in Keep Yard, Bermuda, built between 1837 and 1852 and surrounded by the massive bastioned defences originally designed to deter American attack. Keep Yard is centred on the boat pond for the ammunition boats. In an arrangement unique to Bermuda, where the channel to the boat pond passes through the defences it could be closed by a portcullis. The buildings here now form the heart of the Bermuda Maritime Museum.

Massive construction, comparative isolation from centres of naval activity and their undoubted utility have done much to help ensure survival of many of these magazines, although all except two of the set at Purfleet were demolished in the early 1970s and Marchwood and Tipner face an uncertain future.

The ordnance yards themselves have had a more chequered history. Those at Chatham, Portsmouth and Devonport were adjacent to the dockyards and passed into Admiralty hands after the abolition of the Board of Ordnance. Chatham was sold after the Second World War and its most distinguished building, Vanbrugh's storehouse, was demolished (139). Most of the site is now occupied by the Lloyd's headquarters building, but the former storekeeper's house below St Mary's church was rescued from demolition and is now a public house, while former gun carriage stores are in local authority use.

Downstream on the opposite side of the river Upnor Castle remains along with the early eighteenth-century barracks built to house soldiers guarding the gunpowder. Although convenient to the dockyard, Upnor was atypical and never ideal as a powder store. The main Tudor building, adapted as the magazine, lay at the top of the low cliff above the angled water bastion where the powder boats loaded and unloaded their cargoes (138). A 1750 report by the Surveyor General of Ordnance comments tersely on the somewhat hazardous arrangements then in force there: 'The method now used to lift up the powder barrels into the magazine is by running a rope through a pulley, one end of which is fastened to a powder barrel, and a man taking hold of the other, jumps out of the window . . .' Not surprisingly, the Surveyor General felt moved to comment on the safety, reckoning that this '. . . is a dangerous and uncertain method, for if he is too light, the powder barrel will not ascend, and if he is too heavy, he is sure to bruise himself against the pavement, whereby it is very difficult to get men who will run such a risk upon labourers' pay'. The remedy, which can still be seen, was to install a proper windlass in the magazine, but this was only a partial solution and the castle's general inconvenience goes far to explain its abandonment as a magazine by the board in 1827.

By the late eighteenth century, Portsmouth ranked among the most heavily fortified towns in Europe, its gun wharf lying south of the dockyard. Space here was at a premium, for it served not only the navy but also the land defences. It is now part of HMS *Vernon* and contains only a few buildings from its time as the busiest of all ordnance yards. The most impos-

138. *Above right* At Chatham, the Board of Ordnance used Upnor Castle as a powder magazine from 1668 to the early nineteenth century. Vessels loaded and unloaded powder barrels onto the water bastion; these were stored in the main part of the castle above.

139. *Right* The main ordnance wharf at Chatham lay immediately upstream from the dockyard. Some of its buildings still survive, but these early eighteenth-century warehouses were demolished after the Second World War.

ing, damaged by enemy action in 1941 and threatened with demolition, is the former Grand Storehouse. A massive three-storey pedimented brick warehouse, now lacking one of its wings, it was constructed between 1811 and 1814 as the main general-purpose storehouse on Ordnance Wharf. Until damaged, it was one of the largest of ordnance buildings, in its heyday crammed with everything from gun carriages to slow matches.

A survey of Portsmouth ordnance yard in 1830 conveys some idea of the types of buildings necessary at a major fleet base towards the end of the era of the smooth bore gun firing a solid shot. New Gun Wharf lay south of the original ordnance wharf, separated from the latter by the water defences of Portsea town. It was laid out late in the eighteenth century.

Old Gunwharf

The Grand Armoury
North Store
Stores 8, 9, 10, 11
Sea Storehouse and 2 covered sheds
Battering Train Storehouse
Storehouse for ships' carriages and 3 adjacent sheds
Range of storehouses for ships' stores
Painters' Shop
Range of storehouses
Binding-off shed
Shed for planking
Workshop for gun carriages
House for blocks
House for linch pins
Ordnance office
Shed for painting gun carriages
Watch and engine house

New Gunwharf

Smithy
Sea Armoury
Grand Storehouse
Guard house
Carpenter's shop
Sighting house

Architecturally, the sparse survivals of ordnance buildings at the former gunwharves at Chatham and Portsmouth are partially compensated by the mid-nineteenth-century yard at Bermuda and especially by the early eighteenth-century Morice Yard at Devonport. The latter is the ordnance yard equivalent of Chatham dockyard in the totality of its surviving eighteenth-century buildings (fig. 8, page 134).

The first gunwharf at Plymouth was established on the foreshore below Mount Wise, but this was inconveniently small and remote. In 1717 a search began for a new location and one was eventually found adjacent to the north-west of the new dock-yard. Not until March 1719 were negotiations completed with the landowner, Sir Nicholas Morice, and the 'buttings and boundings' of the site staked out. The land acquired was an irregular rectangle, bounded on the west by the Tamar and on the north by mudflats. The eastern half of the site was part of a rocky promontory about 40 feet above sea level. Plans for the new yard were drawn up by Colonel Lilly,

140. *Above* Polishing cannon balls at Morice Ordnance yard adjacent to Devonport Dockyard in 1855. The pedimented powder magazine of 1743 still remains. Beyond the cannon balls are rows of carronades. Such weapons and their solid shot were obsolete within a year or two of this scene.

141. *Right* Morice Yard, the Officers' Terrace completed in 1723.

142. *Above right* One of the pair of original storehouses at Morice Yard. These have been little altered internally.

143. *Right* The basic design of powder magazines changed little from the early eighteenth century to the phasing out of black powder nearly 200 years later. In the nineteenth century magazines such as this at Bull Point on the Tamar tended to become larger and be sited at more isolated places. In the foreground is the basin which served it.

senior officer for the Plymouth District, assisted by the master builder and master carpenter from the dockyard. Local contractors were engaged to provide building material, but a London stonemason, William Cowley, won the contract for the bulk of the construction work. He was joined by Abraham Curtis, also probably from London, who was responsible for carpentry and joinery.

In 1720 work began with construction of a wharf and two semi-circular basins adjacent to a pair of three-storey warehouses set at right angles to the waterfront. Between the storehouses were two treadwheel cranes; behind them was the original small magazine whose siting was to cause Horneck such worry twenty years later. To gain extra space at waterfront level, the promontory behind was cut back creating room for a smithy, a limekiln and an area of open ground to store gun barrels and their shot.

On the remaining high ground overlooking the centre of the yard, Lilly placed the terrace for senior officials (141). Like all the yard buildings of this first period it was built of dunstone rubble quarried from the site with detailings in granite. Its somewhat eclectic front elevation with a profusion of pilasters, parapets, pediments and lunette windows has echoes in contemporary Board of Ordnance work elsewhere and although Vanbrugh's name has been associated with Morice Yard on stylistic grounds, there is nothing in the construction accounts to link his name with the project. As with dockyard terraces, each house had a long walled garden to the rear. Nearby, Lilly completed his work by constructing a substantial boundary wall round the landward side of the yard. The main gateway, flanked by the two small houses for the labourers and watchmen, was placed near the terrace, while the latter was linked to the lower part of the yard by a monumental flight of steps set into the rock face. Although the different levels within Morice Yard cannot have been altogether convenient, Lilly's careful planning separated the working area from the residences and gave the officers' terrace a magnificent view across the Hamoaze to Cornwall. Within the storehouses Lilly had wooden truckways laid, with the exception of the treadwheel cranes the earliest recorded instance in a government establishment of the partial mechanisation of stores' handling. Morice Yard was completed in 1724 and with the exception of the powder magazine, limekiln and wooden cranes all the original buildings remain (142).

As completed, Morice Yard was clearly designed as a holding depot with limited arrangements for maintenance, and it remained as such throughout its ordnance life. In 1743 a new powder magazine was added, but little further building work took place until the 1770s when additional capacity was needed to match that of the rapidly expanding dockyard. New powder magazines were built up river at Keyham while at Morice Yard itself two small forge buildings were erected below the cliff, probably for the armourer and for general smithing work. Adjacent to one was built a large carriage store. These all remain and were to be supplemented during the Napoleonic wars with a host of temporary wooden buildings, including an artillery hospital, nurses' quarters and further gun carriage sheds. Morice Yard reached a peak of activity in 1813 when along with a depot at Falmouth it was chosen as the principal ordnance supply base for Wellington's army in Spain.

Later in the nineteenth century Morice Yard was to be swallowed up in the enormous expansion of Devonport dockyard, but it has succeeded in keeping its identity and miraculously escaped the bombing which so devastated the rest of Plymouth and Devonport. It is the sole intact eighteenth-century ordnance yard and along with Priddy's Hard at Gosport gives us an understanding of the considerable Board of Ordnance capital investment needed to arm and equip the Royal Navy.

Chapter 8
Naval Hospitals

In 1705 the Royal Hospital at Greenwich, founded by Queen Mary as a thank-offering for the victory at La Hogue in 1692, admitted its first seamen. This, though, was not a hospital in the modern sense of the word but an almshouse of grandiose scale for such poor and needy sailors as had survived the rigours of naval life. And rigours they were. Ships were cramped and insanitary, provisions were monotonous, poor and frequently bad, while shipboard medical skills, if no worse than on land, had to contend with the effects of poor living quarters and diet on the physiques of the patients. Death or wounds in battle were statistically among the least of the hazards facing crews; diseases such as typhus, yellow fever and scurvy exacted a far more terrible toll.

As long as ships of the Royal Navy were confined to home waters where periods at sea were comparatively short, crews tended to remain tolerably healthy. But by the eighteenth century the navy was ranging much further afield as a matter of course. Longer voyages produced crews weakened by poor diets and in no shape to withstand exposure to new tropical and sub-tropical diseases. Sir Cloudesley Shovell's militarily uneventful five month expedition to the Mediterranean in 1703 produced a death toll due to disease of over 1500 men. The remaining seamen were so debilitated that towards the end of the voyage it was becoming difficult to muster sufficient to man the ships. His successor, Sir Jonathan Leake, estimated that of the original 700 crew who sailed his flagship from Portsmouth in January 1704, only 400 remained alive when he called at Lisbon two years later.

At the beginning of the eighteenth century arrangements for caring for sick and wounded seamen had hardly advanced since the days of the Tudors. Every large warship carried a surgeon who did his best within his limited powers, while from the mid-seventeenth century major expeditions sometimes included hospital ships—hastily converted men-of-war with some of their armament removed to give more space below decks. But the great need was for proper nursing ashore. In peacetime arrangements here were in the charge of the Surgeon-General who hired sick quarters at the principal ports and reserved a number of beds at the great London hospitals. War saw the appointment of Commissioners for Sick and Wounded and Prisoners of War, but their role was merely an extension of that of the Surgeon-General. Extra rooms were reserved at inns and ale houses in dockyard towns, more surgeons were appointed and the system of contract care was expanded. This last involved surgeons contracting to care for sick seamen on a per-capita basis and could involve substantial numbers: under Nathaniel Jackson, the Fortune Hospital at Forton near Portsmouth had space for 700 patients by 1713.

Such a system was far from satisfactory. It was inefficient, capable of abuse and led to widely varying standards of care. In 1702 an Admiralty commission investigated the whole subject and reported in favour of constructing proper naval hospitals. The report was rejected, largely on grounds of cost, for sick seamen were officially considered to be exclusively a wartime phenomenon, while the Navy Board saw the report as a personal slur and indignantly refuted its findings.

But developments abroad were forcing change. It might be possible to carry on in England with this ad hoc system, but overseas where need was most acute, such arrangements were not always possible and the Navy perforce had to look after its own. The first naval hospital was established at Jamaica in 1704. Little is known about this and it was probably no more than a series of wooden huts which by 1739 could accommodate only 62 patients. In 1706 a second hospital was opened in Lisbon, almost certainly in a rented building. In both cases it seems probable that fleet surgeons initially provided the skilled manpower until the hospitals could be turned over to contractors. In 1708 Minorca was captured. With the disasters of Sir Cloudesley Shovell's voyage probably still in mind, the Sick and Hurt Board lost little time in sending an agent charged with 'immediately upon … arrival' setting up a hospital. At first, Pierce Griffyth rented accommodation, apparently a convent 'among a great many suttling houses' in Mahon itself, but the longer-term aim was explicit: he was to consult with the senior naval officers as to the best location to build a proper hospital and was to have plans and estimates prepared locally for approval in London.

In 1709 Admiral George Byng and Griffyth produced an estimate of £9,000, a figure which suggests that they had a substantial hospital in mind.

144. An early eighteenth-century view of the first purpose-built naval hospital on an island in Mahon harbour, Minorca.

145. A ground floor ward in Mahon hospital. In the 1770s some 30 sick and wounded would have been crammed into this 22 × 32-foot space. Not surprisingly, the barred windows were there to deter deserters.

146. An aerial view of Mahon hospital, rebuilt with a first floor between 1772 and 1774.

The scheme came to nothing and in due course Byng was superseded by Admiral Sir John Jennings, a resourceful man unimpressed with the rented accommodation. As Griffyth's original instructions had not been cancelled, Jennings used them as his authority to have a second plan and estimate drawn up early in 1711, probably by Captain Latham, a member of the island garrison. In April Jennings signed a warrant for construction although not until June did he forward his scheme to London for approval. He explained this irregularity a year later by stating that had he waited for permission he would have lost the skilled labour force of Catalan and

144

Majorcan workers then finishing the fortifications. Jennings' blind eye to administrative niceties, what much later generations might have called the Nelson touch, resulted in the first proper purpose-built hospital for the Royal Navy. A curmudgeonly Admiralty, however, instead of congratulating him for completing it for almost a third of the original estimate, withheld payment until Jennings had petitioned Queen Anne on behalf of himself and his brother officers in the Mediterranean fleet from whom he had borrowed funds to finance the project (**144**).

The hospital was sited on a small island in Mahon harbour, convenient for ships but difficult to escape from and well clear of the temptations of Mahon town. It consisted of a long single-storey main range with a central chapel flanked on each side by five vaulted wards (**145**). Wings at each end both had a further three wards and terminated in accommodation for the surgeon, senior naval officer and staff. This pioneering building served the navy throughout the first British occupation of Minorca, but neglect during the French interlude from 1756 to 1763 combined with inadequate maintenance led to a partial collapse in 1770. Such was the hospital's importance that it was rebuilt and a first floor added to increase capacity to 1200 beds. This building remained in use, latterly as a Spanish naval hospital, until the early 1960s, but now stands derelict. Although difficult to prove, it is probable that much of the ground floor is Admiral Jennings' work of 1711 (**146**).

For 30 years, Port Mahon hospital remained unique, taking sick and injured seamen from warships at Minorca and the more serious cases from vessels calling at Gibraltar. The latter, lacking a sheltered harbour, remained comparatively unimportant to a navy fortunate to have Port Mahon, but a hospital at Gibraltar would be well placed between Minorca and Lisbon. Hired accommodation at Gibraltar for less serious cases was in any event strictly limited, and by the 1730s voices were agitating for a purpose-built hospital for the Rock. In 1734 three different designs were prepared, but the largest of these was to hold only 160 patients—one warship with sickness on board would have more than filled it—and perhaps not surprisingly nothing was done.

Five years later, the situation had changed. War with Spain was imminent and the Mediterranean fleet was being reinforced; medical facilities at Gibraltar were at a premium. In November 1739 it was recorded that there were 'upwards of 600 sick people in the hospital'—a reference probably to facilities for the garrison—and when Admiral Haddock arrived with a fleet of nineteen ships and 5,027 sailors, he noted that the permanent sick quarters consisted of two sheds with room for 30 patients. In April 1740 Admiral Sir Charles Ogle complained that his sick and wounded were suffering from being accommodated in huts and tents during the rainy season, a report which finally stirred the Admiralty into action.

In 1741 a thousand-bed hospital was authorised and by November craftsmen from Portsmouth dockyard were being recruited for the construction work. Virtually all materials had to be transported from England and by

147. Gibraltar. The old naval hospital, now Staff Officers' quarters.

1746 the building was complete. The hospital was sited a little way in from Rosia Bay, away from the temptations of the town and, more importantly, sheltered from Spanish land batteries by a shoulder of rock. It is a two-storey quadrangle with deep verandas overlooking the courtyard. Originally, wards ran the full width of the ranges but they could be isolated if necessary by using verandas as corridors. Accommodation was certainly more spacious than at Port Mahon, while the project was completed by a boundary wall, porter's lodge and entrance gates on the north side with staff quarters beyond. The hospital was to play a notable part in the great siege 35 years later and was only superseded in the late nineteenth century. It is now naval officers' quarters (147).

The outbreak of war in 1739 was to prove instrumental in establishing proper naval hospitals in England itself. In the thirteen months from August that year, 15,868 sick and wounded were landed from the fleet, the majority at Gosport and Plymouth. The latter town had accommodation for 463 but by the end of 1740 three times that number were being cared for. In February 1740 a 'violent and malignant fever' was introduced into Plymouth by crews from HMS *Panther* and HMS *Canterbury*. The epidemic spread to London where in 1741 more people died of typhus than in any year since the Great Plague. The folly of inadequate care for the navy's sick was becoming obvious to all. Such was the desperation at Portsmouth that in October 1740 the Admiralty suggested using Portchester Castle as a hospital. This was then a prisoner-of-war camp, but the Admiralty felt that the Roman walls would be equally useful in containing the more active patients, while conversion costs of £1,800 to provide a 1,100 bed hospital must surely remain something of a record for government parsimony. Only leasing difficulties prevented implementation of the scheme.

In March 1741 the Commissioners for Sick and Wounded sent a memorandum to the Admiralty in which they estimated that the annual cost of caring for 1,000 seamen at Gosport was £21,516 12s 8d under the existing contract system and £13,879 6s 8d in a navy-built and navy-run hospital. Again, opponents of naval hospitals argued that they would be a needless expense in peacetime, but the following month the Admiralty proposed that two 750-bed hospitals be built at Queenborough in Kent and at Plymouth and a 1,500 bed hospital be built at Gosport. Significantly, the men were to be looked after 'at his Majesty's expense'.

But if financial implications could be endlessly argued by healthy administrators and politicians far removed from the suffering, humanitarian reasons dictated direct control rather than any extension of the contract system. Among the welter of correspondence and memoranda, one report in 1742 is particularly telling. It noted that at the navy-built but contractor-run hospitals at Port Mahon and Gibraltar 'beds are not provided either by the Public or the Contractors . . . which cannot but be attended with great inconvenience to the people who are sent to them, and in all likelyhood with the loss of many who have no beds of their own'.

In spite of the Admiralty proposal of April 1741 for three hospitals, nothing had happened by 1744 when the newly appointed Lord Commissioner of the Admiralty, the 26-year-old Earl of Sandwich, revived the matter. Again, three hospitals were asked for, but Chatham was substituted for Queenborough, and it was said that if money was short £37,000 should

Fig. 9. Haslar Royal Naval Hospital c. 1800.

Key:
1. Entrance
2. Hospital
3. Operating Room etc.
4–5. Staff Houses
6. Chapel of St. Luke
7. Senior Medical Staff Houses
8. Guardhouse
9. Landing Place for sick and wounded

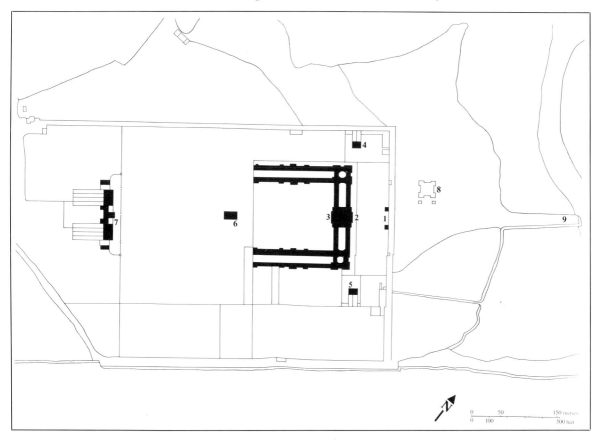

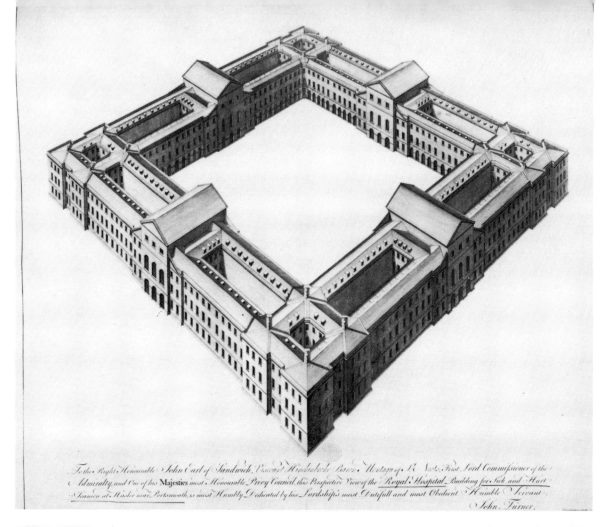

To the Right Honourable John Earl of Sandwich, Viscount Hinchinbrooke, Baron Montagu of St Neots, First Lord Commissioner of the Admiralty, and One of his Majesties most Honourable Privy Council, this Perspective View of the *Royal Hospital* Building for Sick and Hurt Seamen at Haslar near Portsmouth, is most Humbly Dedicated by his Lordship's most Dutifull and most Obedient Humble Servant, John Turner.

be spent on a 1,500-bed hospital at Portsmouth in preference to the other two. This time, an Order-in-Council followed, among other things stipulating that naval hospitals were to be navy-run; contractors were only to be used to supplement the system in wartime and where no navy hospital was available.

After a survey of possible sites, construction of a hospital on the Gosport side of Portsmouth Harbour at Haslar was ordered in June 1745. Although Sir Jacob Ackworth, Surveyor of the Navy, drew up preliminary plans, Haslar Hospital owes its design to Theodore Jacobson, architect of the Foundling Hospital in London, proof of the Sick and Hurt Board's desire to employ the best qualified architect of the day. The chosen site had two advantages: it was near the harbour mouth enabling patients to be landed at its own jetty, but it was some distance from the nearest community, an aid both to containing infection and any infectious or wounded who might be tempted to desert. The foundations were begun in 1746 and the buildings were completed in 1761. The early design was for a series of double ranges each over 550 feet long forming a vast quadrangle (**148**). In the event, the rear range was never built. On the site was put the hospital church of St Luke and, in 1796, this side was closed by a formidable iron railing beyond which lies the terrace housing of the senior medical staff (fig. 9, page 147).

The original 1746 design had been for 1,500 patients; in 1754–5 this was increased to 1,800 and by 1779 2,100 were being cared for. A survey of 1780 showed the hospital with 84 general medical and surgical wards together with consumptive and isolation wards for fever and smallpox. Each ward had its own water closet and there was a bath house for new admissions. Haslar's first physician was the celebrated Dr James Lind, appointed in 1758. He perhaps more than any other man was responsible for raising medical standards in the Royal Navy and it was largely his agitation and that of his fellow physicians Blane and Trotter that forced the Royal Navy in 1795 to start to issue lemon juice as an anti-scorbutic. Significantly, bottling and storage of this juice was first carried out in the cellars of Haslar and Plymouth hospitals. Not until 1812 did the Victualling Board assume the responsibility and cost of this operation. In the 1939–45 war, the Haslar cellars found a new use as operating theatres, while the rest of the hospital has been modernised over the years. Only the blocks at the western end of the southern range still retain a significant part of their original internal arrangements, including the handsome wooden staircase. Over two centuries after its completion, Haslar remains the centre of naval medicine (**149, 150**).

Although the 1744 Order-in-Council had specified three hospitals, Chatham was not to receive one until the nineteenth century. More urgent was one to serve the fleet base at Plymouth, but construction of Stonehouse hospital was not to start until 1758. Following the Gosport precedent, some considerable time had been spent seeing if a local prison could be converted more cheaply. Stonehouse hospital was designed by a Mr Rovehead. Little

148. *Opposite top* An early design for Haslar Hospital, Gosport, the first purpose-built navy-run hospital in England begun in 1746. Only three ranges were built.

149. *Opposite* Haslar Hospital. The great courtyard before the recent link building somewhat changed its aspect.

is known about him, but his work here shows him to have been a competent architect whose design was medically in advance of that of Haslar where the full-width wards had to be used as corridors. At Stonehouse, Rovehead arranged ten three-storey blocks formally round a central courtyard. Interspersed between the blocks were four single-storey pavilions, probably kitchens and mess rooms, and all were linked by a colonnaded passage. The focal point, forming an axis with the main entrance, was the administrative block and chapel, its main elevation provided with a pediment and surmounted by a clocktower and bell cupola (151, 152).

Each block of wards was divided by a spine wall and had a staircase at one end. Originally, patients were ferried in ships' boats up Stonehouse Lake to the hospital jetty. This led directly to a building used as a bath house and clothing store. Washed and issued with clean clothes, the patients were then led to the hospital proper. Stonehouse was smaller than Haslar; its original specification was for 600 patients but this was soon increased to 960. By 1795 1,200 were divided among 60 wards, while another 50 'slight cases' were kept in two cellars.

Haslar and Stonehouse have remained the principal naval hospitals, supplemented in wartime by further accommodation. At the end of the eighteenth century, casualties from squadrons based at the Downs were cared for at Deal, those from the eastern squadron at Great Yarmouth. Both places used rented accommodation, but in 1807 the Admiralty ordered construction of a 300-bed hospital at the Norfolk town. Almost certainly designed by Holl and incorporating a stretcher lift alongside the main staircase, this

150. The main entrance to Haslar hospital in 1942 with its elaborate pediment sculpted by Thomas Pearce. Flanking the arms of George II, on the left the female figure of *Navigation* leans on a rudder and pours oil on a wounded seaman, while on the right *Commerce* distributes money, fruit and flowers. Beyond, a distressed mariner is being succored by a bird carrying in its beak the serpent of Aesculapius.

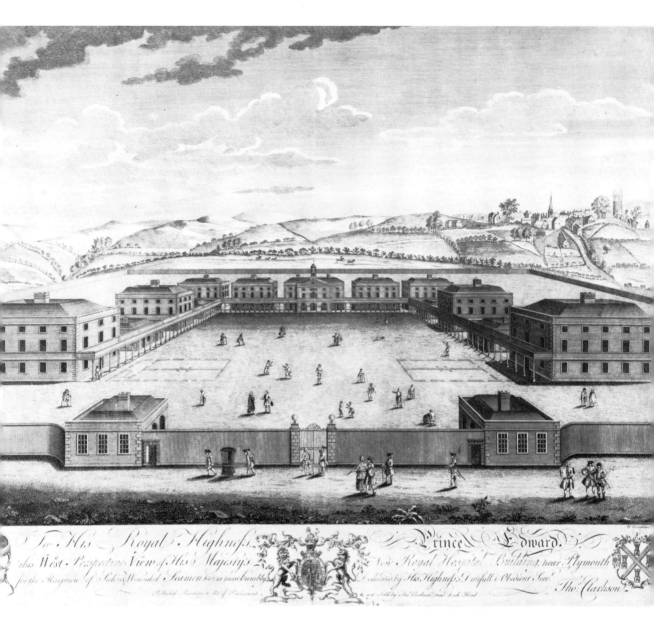

For His Royal Highnefs Prince Edward. this West Perspective View of His Majesty's New Royal Hospital Building near Plymouth for the Reception of Sick & Wounded Seamen &c is most humbly Dedicated by His Highness's Dutifull & Obedient Serv.t Tho.s Clarkson

151. Stonehouse Hospital, Plymouth, begun in 1758. So as not to obscure the view of the courtyard, the artist has shown only the foundations of the two nearest blocks.

echoes on a much smaller scale the Haslar layout. It has long ceased to be a naval hospital and is now a local authority home.

Overseas, it was not until the nineteenth century that further hospitals were constructed to rival the early ones at Port Mahon and Gibraltar. Most remarkable of these later ones is the surviving building at Port Royal, Jamaica. This was largely constructed from cast iron units prefabricated in England and shipped out around 1817. This two-storey structure, nearly 400 feet long, was sufficiently robust to withstand the great earthquake of 1907. It pioneered the use of cast iron on this scale for naval buildings overseas and gave Holl valuable experience which he was to use in the

design of the Commissioner's House at Bermuda.

When the Navy shifted its base of operations from Minorca to Malta in 1802 its nearest hospital lay far to the west in Gibraltar. But Valletta, unlike other overseas bases, had numerous buildings available for rent. For the first 30 years of the British occupation, sick and wounded seamen were cared for either in the former Knights' armoury at Vittoriosa or in the more sinister surroundings of the erstwhile Turkish slave prison in the capital. Such expedients, though, proved costly to adapt and run and in 1818 came the first official suggestion to amalgamate facilities in one building. At first the former Inquisitor's Palace at Vittoriosa was favoured, but fortunately for future patients this grim and airless building proved unsuitable. In the event, an unfinished palace at Bighi was selected. High on a bluff overlooking Grand Harbour with spectacular views across to Valletta, it caught any breeze in the hot summer weather and was convenient to the fleet anchorage.

The Navy employed two local architects, the Xerri brothers, to adapt and extend the palace. The existing building was turned into offices, a chapel and a dispensary. At right angles on either side were constructed two wings raised on massive rusticated basements. At each corner these had small pedimented pavilions for officer patients. By 1840, ten years after its completion, the hospital could accommodate 240 patients, the wards arranged on either side of wide central corridors. It remained in use by the Royal Navy until 1960 and must have been one of the most pleasant of such establishments (154).

Later in the nineteenth century major hospitals were to be built at Chatham and Gibraltar, but by then society had accepted its responsibility to care properly for sick and injured servicemen. It was the pioneering efforts in the eighteenth century, especially in the overseas bases, which deserve to be recorded.

How effective these developments were in lessening mortality and permanent disablement is almost impossible to assess with precision. Seamens' health depended upon adequate diet and shipboard hygiene as well as good medical care, and all were subject to reforms and improvements, often instigated by the same people. Out of the 184,899 sailors serving in the Seven Years War, 1,512 were killed in action but 133,708 were lost through disease and desertion. During the wars at the end of the eighteenth century, the situation improved markedly. Between 1779 and 1813 the death rate among sailors fell from 1 in 42 to 1 in 143, while the proportion of sick fell from 1 in 2·45 to 1 in 10·75. In 1840 Malta hospital was responsible for caring for the more seriously sick among the 10,000 seamen of the Mediterranean fleet. This involved about 800 patients annually, of whom some four per cent died. Such random statistics must be treated with caution, but what is clear is a steady improvement in seamen's health. If Great Britain got off to a late start in the proper care of her sailors, she was still in advance of any other naval power.

152. *Opposite top* Stonehouse Hospital early this century. Although wardamaged, it remains much as completed, and, like Haslar, is a monument to changing Georgian attitudes to caring for sailors of the Royal Navy.

153. *Opposite bottom* Stonehouse Hospital. The terrace for the senior medical staff begun in 1763. Since this nineteenth-century photograph was taken its main elevations have been rendered.

154. *Right* The former naval hospital, Malta, about 1860. Its commanding position above Grand Harbour made it one of the most attractive of overseas hospitals.

Sources

There are very few published works on the development of the Royal Navy's bases; those found to be most helpful are listed below. The overwhelming bulk of information in this book came from manuscript sources chiefly in the Public Record Office and the National Maritime Museum. The list below is of the main classes of documents consulted:

General

Navy Board in-letters from the Admiralty	(PRO) ADM/A/1756–2142
Admiralty in-letters from the Navy Board	(PRO) ADM/1/3629–3643
Navy Board out-letters to the Admiralty	(NMM) ADM/BP/1–40b
	ADM/B/149–235
Bentham papers	(PRO) ADM/1/3525–3527

Navy Estimates 1792–1854 in the *Parliamentary Papers.*

Chatham

In-letters from the Navy Board	(NMM) CHA/E/1–116

Portsmouth

In-letters from the Navy Board	(NMM) POR/A/1–64

Plymouth Dock (Devonport)

In-letters from the Navy Board	(PRO) ADM/174/1–80
Out-letters to the Navy Board	(PRO) ADM/174/113–158

Overseas Yards

Admiralty Dispatches	(PRO) ADM/1/376, ADM/1/383–403
In-letters to the Admiralty	(PRO) ADM/1/3441–3446
In-letters to the Navy Board	(PRO) ADM/106/2043–2052
Gibraltar out-letters to the Navy Board	(PRO) ADM/106/2020–2026

Victualling Board

In-letters to the Victualling Board	(PRO) ADM/109/86–99
Victualling Board minutes	(PRO) ADM/111/255–267
Out-letters from the Victualling Board	(PRO) ADM/114/40–47

Board of Ordnance

Surveyor-General's minutes	(PRO) WO/47/15–120
Board of Ordnance out-letters to Admiralty	(PRO) ADM/1/4007–4027
Miscellaneous	(PRO) WO/55/5–7

Sick and Hurt Board

Minutes	(PRO) ADM/99/1–90
Out-letters to Admiralty	(PRO) ADM/98/1–8
In-letters from the Admiralty	(NMM) ADM/E/5–8b

Maps, plans and architectural drawings
For dockyards, the PRO (ADM/140 series), the National Maritime Museum and the British Library have a large and random selection.
Board of Ordnance material is mainly in the PRO in the WO/55 series.
Bermuda archives contain a selection of drawings relating to Bermuda dockyard.

Printed Sources

Arnell, J.	*The Bermuda Maritime Museum and Royal Naval Dockyard, Bermuda.* Bermuda Press, 1979
Bannister, T.	'The First Iron Framed Buildings'. *Architectural Review*, 107, 1950
Baugh, D. A.	*Naval Administration 1715–1750.* Navy Records Society, 120, London, 1977
Blackburne, Sir K.	*The Romance of English Harbour*, 5th Edition. Friends of English Harbour, Antigua, 1954
Brockman, W. E.	'The Growth of a Naval Base 1795–1932'. *The Royal Gazette and Colonist Daily*, Bermuda, May 1933
Buisseret, D.	*Historic Architecture of the Caribbean.* London, Heinemann, 1980
Coad, J. G.	Chatham Ropeyard. *Post-Medieval Archaeology*, 3, 1969
Coad, J. G.	'Two Early Attempts at Fire-proofing in Royal Dockyards'. *Post-Medieval Archaeology*, 7, 1973
Coad, J. G.	'Historic Architecture of HM Naval Base, Portsmouth 1700–1850'. *Mariner's Mirror*, 67, 1, 1981
Coad, J. G.	'Medway House, Chatham Dockyard'. *Collectanea Historica. Essays in Memory of Stuart Rigold*, ed A. Detsicas. Maidstone, Kent Archaeological Society, 1981
Coad, J. G.	'Historic Architecture of Chatham Dockyard 1700–1850'. *Mariner's Mirror*, 68.2., 1982
Coad, J. G.	'Historic Architecture of H.M. Naval Base, Devonport, 1689–1850' *Mariner's Mirror* 1983, forthcoming.
Collinge, J. M.	*Navy Board Officials 1660–1832.* London, Institute of Historic Research, 1978
Gilbert K. R.	*The Portsmouth Blockmaking Machinery.* London, HMSO, 1965
Lloyd, C. and Coulter, J. L. S	*Medicine and the Navy 1200–1900.* Volume 3, 1714–1815, Edinburgh, E. and S. Livingstone, 1961
MacDougall, P.	*The Chatham Dockyard Story.* Rochester, The Rochester Press, 1981
Pawson, M. and Buisseret, D.	*Port Royal Jamaica.* Oxford, 1975
Pugh, P. D. G.	'The History of the Royal Naval Hospital, Plymouth. *Journal of the Royal Naval Medical Service*, 58, 1972
Revell, A. L.	*Haslar, The Royal Hospital.* Gosport, The Gosport Society, 1978
Sainty, J. C.	*Admiralty Officials 1660–1870.* London, University of London, Athlone Press, 1975
Skempton, A. W. and Johnson, H. R.	'The First Iron Frames'. *Architectural Review*, 119, 1962

Victoria County History of Kent, Volume 2, Maritime History, London, 1926

The Mariner's Mirror, the quarterly journal of the Society for Nautical Research, carries articles on dockyard history. Details from the Hon. Sec., National Maritime Museum, London SE10 9NF.

The Navy Records Society publishes annual volumes covering all aspects of naval history. Details from the Hon. Sec., c/o Royal Naval College, Greenwich, London SE10 9NN.

Post-Medieval Archaeology, the journal of the Society for Post-Medieval Archaeology, carries occasional papers on archaeological and architectural aspects of maritime history. Details from P. J. Davey, Treasurer, Society for Post-Medieval Archaeology, The Institute of Extension Studies, 1 Abercromby Square, PO Box 147, Liverpool L69 3BX.

Sources of Illustrations

British Library:
Plates 1 (Kings Ms 43), 2 (Kings Top. XVI), 3 (Lansdowne 847), 6 (Kings Top), 7 (Lansdowne 847), 40 (Harl. 4318), 45 (Harl. 4318), 80 (Kings 43), 98 (Kings 43), 144 (Kings Top. LXXIV), 148 (Kings Top. XIV), 151 (Kings Top. XI).

National Maritime Museum:
4 (230S), 28 (7932), 37 (ADM/YP/21), 57 (C5774), 58 (C7520/D), 100 (ADM/YP/90), 152 (59/767), 153 (P1263/179), 154 (3836).

Public Record Office:
12 (ADM/140/496), 14 (ADM/140/1316), 17 (ADM/140/1281), 47 (ADM/140/496 pt. 2), 54 (ADM/140/532–1), 66 (ADM/140/260), 70 (ADM/140/110), 72 (ADM/140/111 pt. 5), 78 (ADM/140/107 pt. 3), 84 (ADM/140/522 pt. 2), 87 (ADM/140/270), 90 (ADM/140/86 pt. 1), 114 (ADM/140/68 pt. 4), 132 (WO/55/2269), 133 (WO/55/2269).

National Monuments Record:
46, 65, 134, 135, 139, 150.

Flag Officer, Medway, Photographic Section:
38, 43, 61, 62, 68, 103, 105.

Ministry of Defence:
18, 140.

Crown copyright: Reproduced with the permission of the Controller of Her Majesty's Stationery Office:
5, 8, 9, 10, 27, 30, 31, 34, 36, 38, 39, 41, 42, 43, 44, 49, 50, 51, 53, 55, 60, 63, 64, 67, 68, 71, 74, 75, 76, 79, 81, 82, 83, 85, 86, 88, 89, 93, 95, 99, 101, 102, 106, 113, 116, 117, 118, 119, 120, 121, 122, 123, 124, 125, 128, 136, 137, 138, 141, 142, 143, 149.

Author:
15, 16, 19, 21, 22, 26, 29, 32, 33, 35, 52, 56, 59, 69, 73, 77, 91, 92, 94, 96, 97, 104, 107, 108, 109, 110, 111, 112, 115, 126, 129, 130, 131, 138, 145, 146, 147.

Portsmouth Royal Naval Museum:
20.

Plymouth City Library:
127.

Index

Italic numerals preceding page references indicate plate numbers

HMS *Achilles*, *20*, 43
Ackworth, Sir Jacob, 149
Aden, 19
Admiralty Board, 15, 21
Admirals' houses, *106*
Anchorsmiths, 67
Antigua Dockyard: *18*, 19
   Clarence House, *109*, 104
   Cook house, 108
   Double dock, 20, 55
   Gateway, *97*, 95
   Officers' houses, *108*, *110*, 97, 104–5
   Powder magazine, 136
   Pre-fabricated building, 32
   Sail loft, 69
   Saw pits, *32*, 44
   Smithery, *59*, 67
   Storehouses, *110*, 92
   Victualling store, 117
Apprentice Training centre *see* School for Naval Architecture
Archer, Captain, 135
Armourers' shops, 141
Artillery defences, 16, 105
Ascension Island, 120

Bage, Charles, 90
Baker, 19
Bakery, *121*, *127*, *128*, *131*, 120–4, 127–8
Barns, 108
Basins, *24*, *41*, *121*, *137*, 48, 49, 50, 53, 55, 81, 82
Battle, Sussex, 131
Bentham, Sir Samuel, 23, 35, 79
   collaboration with Brunel, 39
   Dry-dock improvements, 53
Bentham, Jeremy, 23
Bermuda Dockyard, 15, 19, 40, 120
   Boat pond, 136
   Commissioner's House, *112*, 32, 103, 105–8, 152
   Dry-docks, 55
   Floating dock, 55
   Powder magazine, 136
   Sail loft, 71
   Storehouses, 92
   Victualling yard, *26*, 117, 128
Bermuda Maritime Museum, 108, 136
Bermuda Ordnance Yard, 137
Black yarn stores, *71*, 72
Blake, Robert, Admiral, 17
Blane, Sir Gilbert FRS, 149

Blockmakers, *54*
Blockmills, *74*, *75*, *76*, 15, 39, 53, 63, 81
Boat houses, *49*, *50*, *51*, *92*, 64, 89
Boat ponds, *49*, 64, 89
Bombay, 19
HMS *Boreas*, 104
Boschetti, John Maria, 126
Boundaries, *93*, *94*, 93–5
Breweries, *121*, *122*, *127*, 120–4
Brunel, Marc Isambard, 15, 39, 79, 81
Building contracts, 28
Buildings, prefabrication of, 32
Bull Point powder magazine, *143*, 135
Bunce, Samuel, 23
Byng, Admiral George, 143

Cadiz, 17
Caissons, 53
Canal tunnel, 45
HMS *Canterbury*, 146
Capstan makers, *54*
Caribbean, 15, 17
Carpenters, 66
Carvers, 64
Castries *see* St Lucia
Chain pumps, 53
Chapels, *103*, *114*, *115*
Churches, *113*, 109–11
Chatham Dockyard, *1*, *2*, *11*, 16, 17, 19, 34, 40, 67, 116, 129
   Anchor Wharf, 87–8
   Basins, *43*, 49, 82
   Black yarn house, 72
   Boat houses, *52*, 64, 89
   Boundaries, 93
   Chapel, *103*, *114*, *115*, 109–11
   Colour loft, 63
   Commissioner's house, *103*, *104*, *105*, 98–101
   Covered slips, *38*, 46, 48
   Double-dock, 55
   Dry-docks, 49, 53, 55, 82
   Double ropehouse, *68*, *69*, *72*, *73*
   Factory, 82
   Gateway, *94*, 93, 94
   Guard house, *96*
   Hemp store, *62*
   Hospital, 147, 149, 153
   Joiners' shop, 66
   Lead and Paint Mill, *78*, 81
   Machine shops, 48
   Mast houses, *29*, *30*, 43, 66

Mast pond, 90
Mould loft, *29*, *30*, 43, 66
Officers' terrace, *102*, *103*, 66, 94, 96, 108–9
Rigging house, *90*, 87
Ropery – *see* Double ropehouse – *10*, 39, 63, 71, 77, 81, 85, 87
Sail loft, *60*, *61*, *103*, 63, 69, 94
St. Mary's Creek, 82
Sawmills, 77, 39, 45, 81
Sawpits, *82*, 87
Seasoning sheds, *34*, *35*, 45, 46
Smithery, *58*, 63, 68
Spinning house, *63*
Steam engines, 39, 53, 77
Storehouses, *61*, *68*, *81*, *82*, *90*, 83, 87, 88, 89
Tarring house, *70*
Victualling store, 117
Wet docks *see* Basins
White yarn store, *70*
Chatham Ordnance Wharf, *139*, 136
Chilworth, 131
Clarence, Duke of, *see* William IV
Clarence House, Antigua, *109*, 104
Cocoa, 114
Colour loft, 63
Commissioners' houses, *99*, *103*, *104*, *105*, *106*, *107*, *112*, 23, 32, 97–109, 152
Commissioners, out-stationing of, 21
Commissioners for Sick, Wounded and Prisoners of War, 142
Contractors, 25, 121, 126, 140
Cooperages, *119*, 120–27
Cordage – naval requirements, 77–78; end of government production, 77
Cookhouse, 105
Covered docks, 46
Covered slips, *36*, 39, 41, 46
Cowley, William, 140
Cranes, *47*, 140
Curtis, Abraham, 140

Dartmouth, Royal Naval College, 111
Defoe, Daniel, 15, 83
Deptford dockyard:
   Covered slips, 46
   Dry docks, *28*, 17
Deptford, Royal Victoria Victualling Yard, 115–116, 118
Devonport dockyard, *3*, *4*, 16, 19, 34, 40, 129

Black yarn store, *71*, 72
Chapel, 109, 110
Commissioner's house, *99*
Covered slips, *36*, 41, 46, 48
Double docks, *44*
Dry-docks, 15, 50
Foundry, 67
Mast houses, *55*
Mould loft, 43
Officers' terrace, *5*, *98*, *99*, 95–6
Ropery, *67*, 37, 39, 71, 77, 85
Scrive board, 43
Slips, 27
Smithery, 68
Spinning house, *66*
Storehouses, *80*, *87*, 84, 88
Wheel house, 7
Devonport: Morice Ordnance Yard, *140*, 16, 133, 136
Armourer's shop, 141
Crane, 140
Forge, 141
Gun carriage store, 141
Lime kiln, 141
Officers' terrace, *141*, 141
Powder magazines, *140*, 134–5, 140
Storehouses, *142*, 85, 140
Wharf, 140
Wooden railway, 141
Dickens, Charles, 15, 63
Docks, Double docks, *42*, 20, 53, 55
Dry docks, *22*, *40*, *41*, *44*, 15, 19, 20, 41, 48, 49, 50, 53, 55, 59, 60, 81
Floating docks, 55
Dock pumps, 37
Wet docks – *see* basins
Double ropehouse, *64*, *65*
Dummer, Edward, 15, 50, 86

English Harbour – *see* Antigua
Esquimault, 19
Falmouth, 141
Faversham, 129
Fire-proof buildings, 85, 91–2
Fire mains, 39
Fleet, size affecting dockyards, 41
Forton, Fortune Hospital, 143
Foundries, 39, 67, 71

Gardens, 108–9
Gateways, *93*, *94*, *96*, *97*, *118*, *120*, *126*, 122, 141
George, Prince of Denmark, 109
George III, *15*, 19, 21, 67
Gibraltar Dockyard: *15*, 19, 21, 67
Commissioner's house, *107*, 101–02, 108
Dry dock, 59
Expansion of dockyard, 40
Factory, 82
Great Siege, 101
Hospital, *148*, 145–6, 147, 153
Officers' houses, 97
Storehouses, 92
Workmen, 30

Victualling yard, *129*, *130*, 31, 120, 126–28
Giffard, William, 109
Gin distilling, 116
Gosport, Royal Clarence Victualling Yard, 33, 81, 117, 118, 121, 122–23
Bakery, *127*, *128*, 123–24
Brewery, *127*, 123
Cooperage, *119*, 119, 123
Gateway, *126*, 123
Guardhouse, 123
Mill, *128*, 123
Officers' houses, 123
Ovens, 124
Slaughter house, *127*, 124
Steam engine, 123
Storehouses, 123–24
Weevil Yard, 119
Wharf, 124
Windmill, 119
Great Steam Basin, *see* Portsmouth, 2 Basin
Great Yarmouth, hospital, 150
Green, G. T., 46, 82
Green, W, 101
Greenwich, Royal Hospital, 142
Griffyth, Pierce, 143
Gun carriage stores, 141
Gunpowder, storage, problems of, 121

Haddock, N, Admiral, 145
Halifax Dockyard, 19, 21
Commissioners at, 103
Harwich Dockyard, crane, *47*
Haslar Gunboat Yard, 95
Haslar Hospital, *148*, *149*, *150*, 16, 23, 149, 150
Hatchelling house, 72
Hayfields, 108
HMS *Hebe*, 101
Hemp houses, *62*, 72, 85, 86
Henry VII, 16, 19
Highmore, Thomas, 101
Holl, Edward, 23, 32, 68, 81, 90, 96, 107–08, 110–11, 150, 151
Horneck, 133, 140
Hospitals, *144*, *145*, *146*, *147*, *148*, *149*, *150*, *151*, *152*, *154*, 20, 32, 143–153
House carpenters, 64
Howe, Richard Earl Howe, Admiral of the Fleet, 16
Huddart, Joseph, 73

Industrial Revolution, 15
Inspector General of Naval Works, *see* Bentham, Samuel
Ireland Island, *see* Bermuda
Iron and Brass Foundry, 82

Jackson, Nathaniel, 143
Jamaica, *see under* Port Antonio or Port Royal
Hospital, 143, 151
Jennings, Admiral Sir John, 144, 145
Joiners, 64

Karlskrona, 46
Keyham, 135, 141
Kings Cross station, 48

Latham, Captain, 144
Laying houses, 71, 77, 86
Lead and Paint Mill, *78*, 81
Leake, Admiral Sir Jonathan, 142
Leghorn, 126
Lewis, commissioner at Bermuda, 107
Lilly, Col. Christian, 137–38
Lime kiln, 141
Lind, Dr James, 114, 149
Lisbon, 17, 142, 143
Locksmiths, 68
Lutyens, 19

Machine shops, 39, 48, 79
Machine tools, 15
McIntosh, H, 121
Madras, 19
Mahon, *see* Minorca
Malta dockyard, *16*, *17*, 19, 20, 40, 105
Bakery, *131*, 117, 127–28
Chapel, 111
Commissioners at, 21, 103
Dry dock, 20, 55, 59
Factory, *21*, 82
Foundry, 67
Hospitals, *154*, 152–53
Officers' terrace, *111*, 96–97
Ropery, 71
Victualling, 117
Workmen, 30
Marchwood, 135, 136
Marine Guard House, *see* guard house
Marquand, John, 109
Martin commissioner, 101
Mast houses, 79
Mast makers, 64, 66
Mast ponds, 90
Masts, storage of, 90
Master Shipwrights, building activities, 21, 25, 41
Training of, 112, 113
Maudslay, Henry, 81
Medical provision, history of, 142
Mediterranean, 15, 17
Medway House, Chatham, *see* Commissioners' houses
Melville, Robert, First Lord of Admiralty, 122
Mill, *121*, 120–23
Minorca: Port Mahon dockyard, *14*, 19, 31
Boundary, 95
Careening wharf, 31
Hospital, *144*, *145*, *146*, 20, 31, 143–45, 147, 151
Ropewalk, 71
Storehouses, 192
Victualling, 117, 120
Wharves, 31
Montagu, John, second Duke of Montagu, 133

Moorfields, 129
Morice, Sir Nicholas, 137
Morice Ordnance Yard, *see under* Devonport
Mould lofts, 43
Mould makers, 67
Mount Wise, gunwharf at, 137

Naval Academy, *116*, 109, 111–12
Navy Board, 15, 21, 28, 60, 81, 83
    Fear of fires, 39, 77, 85
    Problems overseeing foreign yards, 31
    Problems with size of warships, 33
Nelson, Admiral Lord, 16, 43, 104
New Delhi, 19
New England, 17
North America, 15
North Yard, Devonport, 82

Oarmakers, 79
Officers' accommodation, *98*, *99*, *100*, *101*, *102*, *103*, *111*, *125*, *141*, *153*, 66, 94, 96–109, 122, 124
Offices, *124*
Ogle, Admiral Sir Charles, 145
Ordnance Board, 21
    early history, 129
    Gunpowder supply, 131
Ordnance yards, 15
    functions of, 129
Ovens, 124, 128
Overhead railway, 45
Overseas bases, labour problems, 30
    materials for, 30

Paddington Station, 48
Painted ceiling at Chatham, 101
Painters' shops, 79
HMS *Panther*, 146
Patternmakers, 67
Pay offices, *89*, 39
HMS *Pegasus*, 104
Pembroke Dockyard, 17
    Officers' houses, 96
Plymouth Breakwater, 120
Plymouth Dockyard *see* Devonport
Plymouth, hospital at, 146
Plymouth victualling facilities, 119. *See* Stonehouse, Royal William Victualling Yard
Port Antonio, 19, 32
Portchester Castle, 147
Port Royal, *19*, 19
    Closure, 40
    Hospital, 32, 143, 151
Portsmouth Dockyard, *6*, *22*, 16, 17, 19, 34, 40, 129, 142
    Admiralty House, *106*
    Basin No 1, *41*, *106*, 49, 53
    Basin No 2, *49*, 82
    Blockmills, *74*, *75*, *76*, 15, 39, 53, 63, 81
    Boat houses, *49*, *50*, *51*, 64, 89
    Boat pond, *49*, 64, 89
    Boundaries, 93

Church, *113*, 109
Coaling point, *25*
Commissioner's house, *106*, 23, 101, 108
Covered slips, *37*, *39*, 46
Dry docks, *22*, *40*, *41*, *43*, 19, 49, 50, 53, 81
Dock pump, *45*, *46*
Double ropehouse, *64*, *65*
Factory, 82
Foundry, 67
Gateway, *93*, *118*
Hospital, 147
Naval Academy, *116*, 109, 111–12
North Basin, 53, 81
Officers' terraces, *100*, *101*, 96
Pay Office, *89*, 39, 86
Porter's Lodge, 93
Reservoir, 81
Ropery, 37, 71, 77
Sail loft, 69
School for Naval Architecture, *117*, 112–13
Sheds, 69
Ship Shop, 79
Smithery, 67
Steam engine, *12*, 53, 81
Storehouses, *9*, *53*, *54*, *83*, *85*, *86*, *87*, 25, 43, 85, 88
Taphouse, 69
Water tower, *13*
Wet dock, 40, 41
Portsmouth, Ordnance Wharf (see also Priddy's Hard), 136
    Grand Storehouse, 137
    List of buildings in 1830, 137
Portsmouth Royal Naval Museum, 25
Portsmouth, Square Tower, 133
Portsmouth Victualling facilities, 119 (see also Gosport, Royal Clarence Victualling Yard)
Powder magazines, *132*, *133*, *134*, *135*, *136*, *138*, *140*, *143*, 132–36, 140–41
Priddy's Hard, 16, 133, 135, 141
    Basin, *137*, 135
    Cooperage, 135
    Powder magazines, *132*, *133*, *136*, 135
HMS *Prince of Wales*, 59
Prisoners, civil, use for building works, 28
Prisoners-of-war, use as labourers, 28
Purfleet powder magazines, *134*, *135*, 129, 136

Queene Anne, 31, 145
Queenborough, proposed hospital, 147
Queen Mary, 142

Rennie, John (1761–1821), 15, 55, 90, 110
Rennie, Sir John (1794–1874), 15, 120–22, 123
Riggers, 87
Rigging houses, *90*, 87
Rochester, victualling at, 119
Ropemaking, 71–77
Roperies, *67*, *68*, *69*, *72*, 39, 63, 71, 79, 85, 87

Fires at, 37
Rosyth Dockyard, 17, 19
Rovehead, Alexander, 149
Royal Dockyards, general references, 15, 17
    Finance, 33
Royal Engineers, 15, 25
Royal Sovereign, 101

Sail lofts, *60*, *61*, 39, 69, 71, 79, 94
Sailmakers, 68, 69, 79
St. Budeaux, 135
St. Loe, George, 52, 101
St. Lucia, Fortified Coaling Station, 40
St. Vincent, John, first Earl, 126
Sandwich, Montagu John fourth Earl, 15, 147
Sauerkraut, 114
Sawmills, 77, 15, 39
Sawpits, *82*, 44, 66
Scamp, William, 82, 128
School for Naval Architecture, *117*, 112–13
Science Museum, 81
Scrive Boards, 43
Seasoning sheds, *34*, *35*, 45, 46
Seppings, Sir Robert, 67
Seven Years War, effects on dockyards, 34, 45
Sheds, 69
Sheerness Dockyard, *8*, 116, 120
    Boathouse, *92*
    Chapel, 110
    Joiners' shop, *33*
    Mould loft, *33*,
    Officers' terrace, 96, 108
    Sawpits, *33*, 44
    Storehouses, *91*, 90–1
    Victualling yard, 117, 126
Shipbuilding, 60
Ship shop, 79, 82
Shipwrights, 66, 79
Shovell, Sir Cloudesley, 142, 143
Simonstown, 19
Singapore, 19, 59
Slaughterhouse, *127*
Slips, 43, 60, *see also* Covered slips
Smitheries, *58*, 63, 67, 68
Smiths, 67, 79
Smithsonian Museum, 81
Spinning houses, *63*, *66*, 71, 72, 77, 86
Sprinklers, 39
Steam engines, *12*, 44, 45, 53, 77, 81
    Early limitations, 35, 39
Stonehouse Hospital, 149–50
Stonehouse, Royal William Victualling Yard, 33, 81, 117, 118, 120–22
    Bakery, *121*, 121–22
    Basin, *121*, 121–22
    Brewery, *121*, *122*, 121–22
    Cooperage, 121–22
    Gateway, *120*, 121–22
    Guardhouse, 121–22
    Mill, 121–22
    Officers' houses, *125*, 121–22

Offices, *124*, 121–22
Slaughterhouse, 121–22
Storehouses, *121*, *123*, 121–22
Wharves, 121–22
Storehouses, *31*, *68*, *80*, *81*, *82*, *83*, *84*, *85*,
  86, *87*, *88*, *90*, *91*, *110*, *121*, *123*, *129*, *130*,
  139, *142*, 25, 43, 83
  Late 17th century stores, 84
  18th century improvements, 85
  Overseas storehouses, 91–2
  Types of storehouses, 86–88, 89, 90, 91
  Ordnance Stores, 91–2
  Victualling stores, *121*, *123*, *129*, *130*,
    120–28

Taphouse, 69
Tarring houses, *70*,
Taylor, George Ledwell, 32, 106, 123
Templar and Parlby, contractors, 25
Tilbury Fort, 133
Tipner, 135, 136

Tower of London, 129
Trincomalee, 19
Trotter, Thomas, 149

Unicorn Frigate, *56*
Upnor castle, *138*, 129, 133, 136

Vanbrugh, Sir John, 94, 136, 141
Vernon, Admiral Edward, 16
HMS *Vernon*, 94, 136–37
HMS *Victory*, *48*, 25, 41, 43, 49, 88
Victualling Board, 81
  Early history, 115–16
  Work of, 118–19
Victualling stores, *121*, *123*, *129*, *130*,
  120–28
Victualling yards, general, 15

Waltham Abbey, 129
Warships, construction of, 41
Weevil Yard, *see* Gosport, Royal Clar-
  ence Victualling Yard
Whale oil, 85
Wharves, 31, 121–22, 124, 140
Wheelwrights, *54*
White yarn stores, *70*, 72
William Henry, Prince, *see* William IV
William IV, 101, 104, 122
Windmill, 119
Wooden truckways, 141
Woolwich Dockyard, 17, 116
  Closure, 39
  Covered slips, 46, 48, 82
  Ropery, 77

Xerri brothers, Salvador and Gaetano, 153

Yard porters, 95
Yarn stores, *see* Black yarn stores and
  White yarn stores